SUFFER THE CHILDREN UNTO ME

SUFFER THE CHILDREN UNTO ME

An Open Inquiry into the Clerical Sex Abuse Scandal

Michael W. Higgins & Peter Kavanagh

NOVALIS

© 2010 Novalis Publishing Inc.

Cover design and photography: Ingrid Paulson
Layout: Audrey Wells

Published by Novalis

Publishing Office
10 Lower Spadina Avenue, Suite 400
Toronto, Ontario, Canada
M5V 2Z2

Head Office
4475 Frontenac Street
Montréal, Québec, Canada
H2H 2S2

www.novalis.ca

Library and Archives Canada Cataloguing in Publication

Higgins, Michael W.
    Suffer the children unto me : an open inquiry into the clerical sex abuse scandal
/ Michael Higgins & Peter Kavanagh.

ISBN 978-2-89646-233-9

    1. Child sexual abuse by clergy--Press coverage--Canada.
2. Mass media--Canada. 3. Catholic Church--Canada.
I. Kavanagh, Peter, 1953- II. Title.

BX1912.9.H54 2010   261.8'327208828271   C2010-905954-9

Printed in Canada.

Directly quoted material, paraphrases and distillations from previous work by Michael
W. Higgins to be found in *My Father's Business* (Macmillan, 1990), *The Jesuit Mystique*
(Macmillan, 1995), *Sex and Marriage in the Catholic Tradition* (Novalis, 2001), *Power and Peril:
The Catholic Church at the Crossroads* (HarperCollins, 2002), and "A Sickness in the Church,"
The Literary Review of Canada (October, 2004) are found periodically in the text.

Excerpts from *From Pain to Hope*, copyright © Concacan Inc., 1992. All rights reserved.
Reproduced with permission of the Canadian Conference of Catholic Bishops, www.
cccb.ca.

We acknowledge the financial support of the Government of Canada through the Book
Publishing Industry Development Program (BPIDP) for our publishing activities.

5   4   3   2   1   14   13   12   11   10

Acknowledgements

For several decades now, we have worked together on numerous projects, media undertakings and joint commissions and have shared a deep and abiding interest in and fidelity to the Roman Catholic faith. As commentators, journalists and public intellectuals, we have struggled to address the many challenges facing Catholicism in our time with integrity, curiosity and fair-mindedness. The current crisis in which the Catholic Church finds itself embroiled has motivated us to bring an analytical and professional perspective to the complex array of factors that make up this crisis.

What follows is the result of our collaborative labour.

It would not have been possible without the assistance, inspiration, encouragement, learning, wisdom, solidarity and love of the following: Paul Baumann, Kevin Burns, Tony Cernera, Sam Dowd, Douglas R. Letson, Bernie Lucht, Robert Mickens, Ami Neville, D. Schmidt (R.I.P.), our many friends and colleagues at St. Thomas University, Fredericton, New Brunswick, and Sacred Heart University, Fairfield, Connecticut.

Most important, of course, is our indebtedness to our long-suffering spouses, Debi and Krystyna.

Contents

1

Bishop Lahey's Bad Day,
A Church's Continuing Nightmare

The picture says it all. An older man, in his late 60s, walking towards a police station, dressed in an open-collared blue shirt, checked sweater and windbreaker. His eyes have the near metaphorical look of a deer frozen in the glare of headlights. Unseen is the crowd of journalists, photographers, cameramen and curious onlookers. He is haunted, hunted, trapped, cornered and on the edge of panic, flight, despair and resignation. He appears isolated and alone, even in the company of lawyers. Solitary but not alone, he is just one element, a temporarily important element, in a much larger tale. His role in the story is just beginning, at a tragic end and ultimately but a snippet in a much larger tale.

Bishop Raymond Lahey may well be the least likely individual to be caught up in the maelstrom that is the sexual abuse scandal rocking the Catholic Church at the end of the first decade of the 21st century. A scholarly intellectual with a credible if not stellar record as a bishop, Lahey had served his Church well over the decades. Born in Newfoundland and educated at Canadian universities, he had done yeoman work in the fields of Church history, liturgy and music. Early in his career and late in his career he had been challenged to take a role in dealing with clerical sexual abuse. That he became a near caricature for the same is irony in operation.

*

We all know the drill; we've seen it thousands of times on TV and at the movies. It would have made for a riveting first five minutes of *Law and Order* or *The Border*: bits of information, troubled glances on the part of law enforcement officials, arguments among investigators and a suspect looking uneasy. The sequence simply needs a hard-driving soundtrack and the audience knows trouble is brewing. Short of a twist in the plot, the investigators are the good guys, the shifty-looking suspect on a narrative arc to the justice he deserves. But that's drama; this is real life, and narrative arcs can be a truly tricky issue.

By all accounts, September 15, 2009, should have been an ordinary day for Raymond Lahey. Arriving on an Air Canada flight from London, England, at Ottawa's Macdonald-Cartier International Airport, the 69-year-old Bishop of Antigonish presented himself at the Canada Border Service (CBS) counter staffed by border services agent Venessa Fairey.

His passport indicated that Lahey had, over time, visited Indonesia, Thailand and Malaysia, all known locations for "sexual tourism." His occupation was evident.

Agent Fairey, in what may be the most startling case of profiling ever, asked if Bishop Lahey had a laptop. She swore that he was evasive, hesitant and unable to make eye contact and then, "voice cracking," said yes. An ordinary day was about to go terribly wrong.

Fairey directed him to CBS agent Caroline Barnett for a follow-up inspection. Barnett performed a preliminary examination of his Toshiba laptop. Finding images she thought might be child pornography, she phoned the Ottawa police.

Two police detectives questioned the bishop, examined the images flagged by Agent Barnett, and seized the computer before allowing Lahey to go on his way. The bad day was about to turn into a legal nightmare that would rock the nation, the Canadian Catholic Church and Catholics worldwide.

For eight days, the Ottawa police wrestled with whether the images identified by Agent Barnett were truly child porn and whether they had sufficient evidence to lay a charge. Canada Border Services agents continued to examine the computer files; they found additional materials that they described to police officers as troubling.

On September 23, the Ottawa police sought a search warrant to "further search the computer and hard drive." Finding what has been described as "hundreds of files and dozens of videos showing young males engaged in sex, some 964 photos," police laid charges of possession and importation of child pornography and issued an arrest warrant.

On September 26, Raymond Lahey resigned as Bishop of Antigonish. In a statement to Catholics of the archdiocese, he claimed he was stepping down for "personal reasons and after much thought and careful consideration." No one seemed to know where he had gone. For days, parishioners and Catholics around the country were confused, and speculation was rife.

On September 30, the fact that an arrest warrant had been issued became public. Canada's news networks were humming with excitement. Banner headlines screamed, "Canada-wide Arrest Warrant Issued for Bishop."

On October 1, Bishop Lahey, accompanied by his lawyer, Michael Edelson, went to the Ottawa police station and surrendered to the authorities. Later that day, he was released on bail. Though his first court appearance was scheduled for November 4, Raymond Lahey and the country were about to discover that we live in an impatient age. Well before that procedural hearing was to be held, Raymond Lahey, and the Church he would come to embody, were going to be assessed, pondered over, judged and found wanting.

The initial media reaction was one of overkill. Every possible incident of clerical sexual abuse worldwide was dragged into the coverage. Interviews were done with Vatican observers live from Rome, where the seemingly key question was "What did the pope know and when did he know it?" The media's default assumptions were that Lahey was an evil man on par with the most egregious of sexual predators, that the enforced celibacy of priests was the explanation for why he had allegedly turned to pornography, that priests were a group more prone than others to sexual crimes, and that the Church, whatever and whoever that meant, would attempt to cover up the full nature of the crime and the hierarchy's complicity in it.

We live in the age of media. News, fact, innuendo, rumour, opinion, slant, spin, perspective, vitriol, conspiracy, confession, accusation and denunciation stream at us through our phones, e-mail accounts, television screens, newspapers, magazines and our walks through life surrounded by monitors spewing out information – benign, assertive and demanding. We are ruled by the codes, routines, demands and grammar of the immediate. In this universe of story, all stories take on an eerie resemblance.

Stories have been with us since the beginning. They serve a variety of purposes and follow some basic rules. The best stories are rooted in individual detail with universal meaning and are told in a style that entertains, captivates, enlightens and elaborates. Through the ages, different types of stories have captured the flavour of the times, becoming barometers of the predominant moods. At the beginning of the 21st century we grapple with several story types: celebrity antics, terrorist threats, government ineptitude, institutional corruption, corporate and individual greed. But sex and crime are two of the most vibrant staples of mass media production and consumption. A firestorm of media attention results when as many elements as possible are mixed together. What arguably works best is if shock, stun, prurience and horror can be melded into familiarity and affirmation of existing prejudices and stereotypes.

Default assumptions tend to be lazy thinking and often contrary to existing evidence. It's a sad commentary that the saying "Don't let the facts get in the way of a good story" has over 27 million citations in a Google search. It is often said of war that truth is the first casualty; it could be equally said, concerning a media frenzy, that nuance, perspective and withholding judgment are among the first virtues to be sacrificed.

*

The irony is that in the weeks before Raymond Lahey's dramatic arrest, victims of sexual abuse were feting him as a hero.

In August of 2009, the Diocese of Antigonish announced an unprecedented settlement of $13 million to compensate for acts of sexual abuse committed in the diocese since 1950. This astonishing move would later prove to be both welcome and bitterly resented. At the moment of the announcement, it was seen as the writing of the final chapter on a remarkably sordid event.

When Raymond Lahey was installed as Bishop of Antigonish on April 5, 2003, he became the shepherd of a flock troubled and divided by accusations that it had been ravaged by men who can be described as sexual predators cloaked in the robes of priests.

According to lawsuits launched against the diocese and Bishop Lahey in 2003, over a dozen individuals had experienced abuse at the hands of at least six priests over nearly six decades. The class action suit came into being at the instigation of Ron Martin, who had been abused as a boy by Father Hugh Vincent MacDonald (who died in 2004), as had his brother David. When David committed suicide in 2002, Ron decided that the pain had gone on too long. As he and his lawyers brought together other victims and began to meticulously document the abuse they had suffered, Bishop Lahey led the campaign within the Church to find some means of resolving the issue without subjecting the victims to even more pain and trauma.

At an understandably emotional public announcement of the settlement, presided over by both the bishop and Ron Martin, Bishop Lahey said, "I was very eager, from the very beginning, to have a conclusion that was as quick as possible, and a conclusion that was as fair and respectful to the victims as possible. I can say for myself that it was clearly something that was wrong, and we wanted to right the wrongs as much as we could do ... I think, to put it very bluntly, we were called upon to do the right thing and to deal with the realities that were there, and to recognize that this is, really, an abuse."

According to many of the victims, as important as the financial settlement was the public apology that Lahey made. "I want to formally apologize to every victim and to their families for the sexual abuse that was inflicted upon those young people who were entitled instead to the trust and protection of priests of the church. I want them to know how terribly sorry we are, how wrong this abuse was, and how we are now trying to right these past wrongs."

When he made the apology to the victims of sexual abuse in the Antigonish diocese, it wasn't the first time he had had to confront the question of clerical sexual abuse. Raymond Lahey was born in St. John's, Newfoundland, in May of 1940. He was ordained in 1963 and spent much of his Church career in positions of increasing responsibility and prestige in Newfoundland dioceses.

Newfoundland was ground zero for the initial Canadian experience of clerical sexual abuse. As "the Scandal" was erupting throughout the United States, rumours and accusations of similar crimes were rapidly becoming rife in Canada, and at the time the old standby rule of Canadian vs. American realities was taking hold. We always assume that, given that we have 10% of the American population, other things being equal we would experience what Americans experience, though at a small total level.

In 1989, the long-rumoured and supposedly much investigated sex abuse scandal at the Mount Cashel Orphanage in St. John's, Newfoundland, was truly revealed. The 90-year-old institution, established and operated by the Irish-based Christian Brothers, had been the site of systemic and constant abuse of young boys by a lengthy list of employees, some of whom were priests. The attitude towards and suspicions of Roman Catholic priests in Canada did a 180-degree shift.

To suggest that no one in the Catholic Church in Newfoundland escaped the impact of the Mount Cashel revelations, the subsequent two inquiries, a best-selling exposé by journalist Michael Harris, and the thinly veiled film dramatization of the whole sordid experience, *The Boys of St. Vincent*, is in one sense to state the obvious. On the other hand, it is impossible to overstate the impact Mount Cashel has had on the perception of the degree of sexual abuse by clerics, the record of the Catholic Church in Canada to wrestle with the consequences of clerical sexual abuse, the self-identity of Catholics and clerics, and the ongoing struggle to understand the narrative that is underway whenever we talk about clerical abuse. In the context of Bishop Lahey, the impact of Mount Cashel was to be immediate as well as long-term.

*

Talking about, testifying over, recounting fully the details of any sexual abuse scandal has always proven to be difficult. Witnesses, victims and alleged perpetrators obviously have distinct and different perspectives. Unfortunately, accounts, evidence and chronologies are all affected by the time between the abuse and the investigation. Canada is not alone in having had to wrestle with the vagaries of memory, the sensitivities of forceful examination of witnesses/victims, as well as shifting definitions of abuse and pornography.

Equally confusing have been the instances of witch hunts around claimed cabals or conspiracies of sexual abuse. The public and the Church are still attempting to wrestle with, integrate and understand what, if any, lessons need to be learned from the residential schools tragedy or the nearly 20-year nightmare behind the alleged Cornwall sexual abuse ring.

The history of the Indian residential schools and the role of the Church in causing, abetting or enabling physical, psychological and sexual abuse is heartbreaking. In the chapter dealing with apologies, we'll explore some of the more difficult issues involved.

The Cornwall situation is at the other extreme of the story of clerical sexual abuse. For nearly two decades, rumours and allegations have circulated and charges laid in connection with a supposed sex abuse ring that operated in the Ontario city of Cornwall. Some went so far as to suggest that the Children's Aid Society, priests, police and senior members of the community's legal and business community conspired to abuse children and then cover up the abuse. Individual cases of abuse became entangled in these allegations, and a near hysteria about the existence of a ring and organized abuse erupted.

The record of police investigations, charges subsequently dropped, lawsuits begun and let lapse is so complex that it cost the Ontario government nearly $50 million to conduct a four-year inquiry. It concluded that it was impossible to say there was ever a sex ring, but that certain institutions, including the Church, had failed to properly address the needs of children claiming to be victims of abuse. The diocese immediately apologized for any and all failings.

Cornwall's 'organized sex ring' is not quite an urban myth, but it does feed into that general sense that the Church as an institution is systemically involved in abusing children. That general sense is alive and functioning in the world today.

*

Child pornography as a crime in and of itself has a relatively short history in Canadian law, and in law worldwide. The history of pornography is in fact largely tied into shifting and evolving ideas of free expression. We have reviewed numerous court cases, royal commissions and human rights hearings in an attempt to sort out conflicting understandings of expression, the nature of sexual depiction and the limits on authorities to interfere with the thoughts as opposed to the deeds of adults. But if we are confused about pornography in general, there is for the moment something of a consensus on child pornography. The operating theory is that children cannot consent to taking part in the production of pornography and are by definition victims.

Section 163.1 of Canada's Criminal Code deals with child pornography. In an analysis prepared by the Library of Parliament of the evolution of pornography law in Canada, Lyne Casavant and James R. Robertson summarize the law, the consequences and the definitions. It prohibits the production, distribution and sale of "child pornography," and also makes it an offence to possess such material. Maximum sentences of ten years for its production and distribution, and five years for simple possession, are prescribed. The section contains a definition of child pornography that includes the following:

> Visual representations of explicit sexual activity involving anyone under the age of 18 or depicted as being so; other visual representations of a sexual nature of persons under the age of 18; and written material or visual depictions that advocate or counsel illegal sexual activity involving persons under that age.

While the law seems clear, the extent and the nature of the problem is a matter of some dispute. There are some estimates that as many as 65,000 Canadians possess or distribute child pornography.

Whereas the reported 964 images found on Lahey's laptop seems large, in February of 2010, a 46-year-old Canadian soldier in Essex, Ontario, was sentenced to one year in jail for possession of 24,000 child pornography images.

Complicating what is already a sad story is that this may not be the first time Raymond Lahey has been accused of possessing pornographic images.

*

During the unfolding public examination of Mount Cashel in the late 1980s and early 1990s, Raymond Lahey was a priest at St. Peter's Parish in Mount Pearl, Newfoundland. In addition to his pastoral duties, he was assisting the diocese in dealing with victims and alleged perpetrators of abuse at that school. According to news reports in 2009, one of the most prominent victims of the abuse at Mount Cashel, Shane Earle, claimed he had seen images of child pornography in Lahey's residence all those years ago.

Earle asserts he was shocked; years later, after Raymond Lahey was appointed Bishop of the Diocese of St. George's in Newfoundland, Earle told another priest, Kevin Molloy, about the incident. Molloy has said he immediately approached Archbishop Alphonsus Penney about the allegation and then informed Lahey of what he had done. Molloy believed at the time, as did Earle, that appropriate measures would be taken.

Shane Earle was living in Halifax when he witnessed the dramatic announcement of the historic settlement announced in August of 2009. He told media that he was impressed and comforted by Lahey's role in forging the historic settlement. When news of Lahey's arrest and charge broke, Earle went public with the story of his encounter decades earlier with the priest he had trusted as a young man attempting to come to grips with his own experiences of abuse. Earle was not the only person to assume that Lahey was guilty as charged and, by definition, the latest in a sad litany of abusing clerics.

*

A presumption of innocence is a legal concept that largely sets the terms of any criminal prosecution. The crown is required to prove beyond a reasonable doubt that the accused has committed the offence charged. The Lahey story is a critical example of how easily the public and the press move past a presumption of innocence to an acceptance of guilt. It is also a window into the shifting sands of what we mean by abuse and how we characterize its consequences. The Lahey affair has become part of shifting attitudes towards the Church, the priesthood, sexuality and the blurring lines between being guilty and been seen as guilty.

*

The day after charges were laid against Lahey in Ottawa, the evolving position of the Church began emerging. Father Tom Rosica, the CEO of Catholic Salt + Light Television, issued this statement:

> The Church throughout Canada is shocked at the startling revelations about Bishop Raymond Lahey, former Bishop of the Diocese of Antigonish. As you know, Bishop Lahey is now in custody in Ottawa, having been charged criminally for possession of child pornography. Bishop Lahey is known to viewers of Salt + Light as a kind and gentle pastor, particularly sensitive to the needs of those who have suffered the scourge of sexual abuse. Those very victims are feeling re-victimized now in light of the events of the past days.

That week, Archbishop Anthony Mancini of Halifax sent a pastoral letter to all the parishes of Nova Scotia. The letter was anguished and clear:

> What do you say to the parishioners, to the priests, the young people and to the faithful communities that make up our Church in Nova Scotia? What will you say to the victims of sexual abuse, as we all struggle in the aftermath of unbelievable revelations and allegations of even more unacceptable shocking and possible criminal sexual behaviour?
>
> What I want to say is: Enough is enough! How much more can all of us take? Like you, my heart is broken, my mind is confused, my body hurts and I have moved in and out of a variety of feelings especially shame and frustration, fear and disappointment, along with a sense of vulnerability, and a tremendous poverty of spirit. I have cried and I have silently screamed, and perhaps that was my prayer to God: Why Lord? What does all this mean? What are you asking of me and of my priests? What do you want to see happen among your people? Is this a time of purification or is it nothing more than devastation?

Two weeks later, at the annual meeting of the Canadian Conference of Catholic Bishops, the outgoing president of the Conference, Archbishop James Weisgerber of Winnipeg, offered the reflections of the bishops: "As bishops we are united in concern and prayer for each other and for all of those whose lives are impacted by the crime and sin of sexual exploitation and sexual abuse," he said. "These include the victims and their families; the local community and society in general; the Christian community in a special way; and also the perpetrators, as well as anyone who has been accused, whether justly or unjustly."

In January of 2010, at the installation of Brian Dunn as the new bishop of the Antigonish diocese, the position of the Church was made clear.

> We gather today as a family of faith experiencing a tragedy. The recent resignation of Bishop Lahey in the midst of the charges of possession of child pornography has created a scar on this diocese and on the whole church. As with any tragedy, our hearts are heavy and we are filled with sadness, disappointment, shock and disillusionment. But this situation has filled us with even deeper emotional responses of anger, resentment, betrayal and outrage. The whole situation has rocked the foundations of our faith and has immersed us in an atmosphere of distrust, suspicion and second-guessing. As your new bishop, I come here to be with you and I count on you to be with me. I bring to you what I have: my firm commitment to listen to you and to receive your stories. During the next few months, I plan to listen to each priest and to the religious and parishioners of each area of the diocese.

There is a unity, a sameness and a sense to the positions offered by different members of the Canadian Church. On the one hand the Church rightly wants to be and wants to be seen as caring first of all for the injured in the alleged crime. Equally, the Church is clearly shocked that one more member of the clergy, a senior member at that, is enmeshed in a crime of shocking dimensions. Finally, there is a recognition that the Church is fighting a battle that has numerous front lines of varying complexions and complications.

*

There are actually four Raymond Laheys in this story.

There is Raymond Lahey the man: mortal, his career in tatters, and his guilt still to be determined. For the media, the world at large, he is the least interesting, the one we all ultimately will attend to only briefly and simply in terms of his legal fate.

There is Raymond Lahey the priest and bishop, the respected academic and scholar, the expert in liturgy and music, the public persona so at odds with the nature of the criminal charges he faces.

There is Raymond Lahey the public face of the Church, who toiled at tasks mysterious to the multitude. He was swept up for decades in attempting to reconcile his ministry and faith with unrelenting evidence of a continuing, unfolding scandal that seems at its heart to violate everything his collar represented.

And there is Raymond Lahey the symbol of a problem that troubles the faithful everywhere.

Making sense of the last two Laheys is what naturally flows from Raymond Lahey's bad day.

*

Think of Bishop Lahey's story as a starting point, an entry into a very confusing, perplexing and troubling situation confronting the Catholic Church today. At any point in our lives, we can be presented with a complex and layered reality that demands that we appreciate, comprehend and come to terms with it in a manner true to who we are. But we need an anchor, a pivot point around which questions can be formulated, facts determined; perspectives assessed; conclusions, both tentative and firm, drawn. The bishop's troubles are just such a fulcrum.

As we will see, the pornography charges against Raymond Lahey were just one facet of a multi-faceted problem that has rocked the Church at its very core in the early years of the 21st century. It's not the first time that sex, power, corruption and matters of loyalty, conscience, belief and faith have come together in a fashion designed to worry the most fervent of us all. And, unfortunately, odds are it won't be the last time. The Church is both divine and human. It is a vehicle of redemption and an institution faced with true temporal problems and consequences.

The reality is that the problems wrapped up in the Lahey story are truly complex, with links and threads knotted in media coverage, social mores, cultural realities, legal procedures, theological understandings and institutional demands. No one issue or solution is to be easily or readily found. No one issue or solution exists that encompasses all that is bound up in the idea of clerical sexual abuse.

What we intend to shape in subsequent chapters is a mosaic captured in the best and most open sense of an inquiry. We'll ask questions, muse on circumstances, reflect on the Church and the world it lives in, trying in all cases not to answer the dilemmas generated by the sex abuse scandal but instead to cast light, disperse shadows, open further inquiries and pose possibilities of understanding.

What we attempt in this book is to explore the history of the modern sexual abuse scandal from a number of perspectives. Chapter Two, "A Canadian Mosaic of Misery – But Not Entire," chronicles the history of the Canadian Church's experience with clerical sex abuse – the crises, cases and constructive (and otherwise) responses. Chapter Three, "A World in Flames," outlines the salient features of the larger turmoil, while Chapter Four, "What We Actually Mean When We Talk About Abuse," explores the paradoxes and turmoil of defining what exactly is at the heart of the problem. Chapter Five, "Constructing the Narrative," moves through the various ways a story is told and how different people and institutions attempt to frame the issue of, and therefore the response to, clerical sexual abuse. Chapter Six, "The Crisis and the Response," explores the international ramifications of the Irish meltdown, the Austrian aftershocks, and the papal and episcopal counter strategies. Chapter Seven, "The Struggle for Narrative: The Language of Apology," is a meditation on the adequacy and inadequacy of apologizing and reconciling. Chapter Eight, "The Heart of the Matter," examines the numerous initiatives, challenges and ongoing problems as the Church plans the recovery of its credibility and the revivifying of its gospel witness.

This book is not the definitive answer for or analysis of the clerical abuse scandal. Answers and analyses will flow over the years from a Church-wide process of reflection, contemplation and decision-making. What we hope to provide is a centre of perspective that allows readers to descend into some deeply troubling and pressing conundrums.

No one book can ever capture the essence of the struggle that the Church and its members are facing.

No one book or even a library of books should be able to do so.

The clerical sexual abuse scandal demands much of the Church and its members. The urgency and depth of those demands cannot be addressed by any single effort. What is clear from the anguished cries of confused parishioners through to the actions, prayers, letters and homilies of Pope Benedict XVI is that the scandal touches every part of the Church, and that every part of the Church needs to be involved in the process of understanding, healing, reconciliation and redemption. It is not an easy process, and no one should be fooled into believing it will be. Some will argue that the solution is simple. Change this or address that and the problem will go away. These simplistic observations are often uttered without any reflection on exactly what is the nature of the problem or what truly is the relationship between the proposed solution and the scandal at large.

Simple solutions are not the stuff of this book. This is a genuine inquiry, an essay into a grievous problem that requires first and foremost perspective, understanding and a willingness to dwell among contradictions and conundrums. For it is in wrestling with the horns of the dilemma, in embracing the perplexities, that we might just find the beginning point of wisdom.

2

A Canadian Mosaic of Struggle

It was an auspicious night, a night of celebration, schmoozing, political showcasing, ecclesiastical fundraising and highbrow social networking. The annual Cardinals' Dinner in the Archdiocese of Toronto was the invention of Gerald Emmett Cardinal Carter. Actually, he stole the idea early in his career as Bishop of London in the late 1960s from his close friend John Dearden, the Cardinal Archbishop of Detroit, but the genesis doesn't matter. What matters is it worked, big time.

The Cardinals' Dinner not only provided an opportunity for Carter to raise money – which it did, and quite successfully – it also provided him with a platform. The Dinner was him.

As John Fraser, Master of Massey College, author, critic, memoirist, irrepressible bon vivant and committed Anglican churchman, rightly observed in *Telling Tales* (Collins, 1986, p. 211),

His Eminence is no less than his grandeur as a cardinal-archbishop. This is a man who enjoys his high office: its trappings, its power, its potential for leadership, its effect on other people .... He also enjoys the company and hospitality of those who wield power and control vast sums of money. If it is true that it is easier for a camel to get through the eye of a needle than for a rich man to gain entrance to heaven, it is also true that if His Eminence has any say in the matter – and I do not rule it out entirely – then at the Gates of Paradise, needles will stand 60 meters high, and their eyes will be sufficiently wide, not just to allow for the passage of dromedaries, but a few Rolls-Royces as well.

He loved the setting. He thrived on the adulation. He was among his people, even if he was actually the son of working-class Montreal parents. He was, after all, by dint of talent, charm, ambition and connection, the right man at the right time for an ever more confident church.

He always chose the annual dinner as an occasion to gently ruminate, crack jokes, display his homiletic skills and, when appropriate, enlighten. He never used it as a forum to rant. Except this time, the dinner of November 8, 1989, his last prior to relinquishing his authority as Ordinary to his successor, Aloysius Ambrozic, on March 17, 1990. This time would be different.

During his address, Carter struck a melancholy, spirited but atypically incoherent note when he covered leadership, hierarchical competence and media persecution in one sour diatribe. He excoriated the media – ordinarily he was the one Canadian prelate who felt comfortable in their world – for failing to appreciate the demands of leadership and for paying servile attention to that most ephemeral of idols: popularity. He thundered,

> The media, particularly the CBC, spearheaded by *The Journal*, have been enjoying a field day with scandals in the Church. I have commented in other ways on the scandals themselves. But I am equally distressed by the ravenous hunger to exploit them in order to denigrate the leadership in the Church. Recently *The Journal* held a panel of several people, one a priest who had deserted his life commitment twenty years ago, another a woman who obviously had an axe to grind, and so on. No one person was invited who was prepared to point out some obvious facts in defense. A kangaroo court and not the first on the CBC. Among other things, the Church was described on the program as a "Gulag." In twenty-seven years as a bishop in the Church, I have never observed repressive measures. There are consultative organisms in every step of governance, much more than in civil government. True, the Church is not a democracy in the sense that our leaders are elected by popular vote. They are chosen by the pope after a wide consultation which includes lay people. And all in all, with due humility, when I look at the bishops and compare them to the House of Commons, I don't feel any inferiority.

He made his point to a captive and respectful audience and all applauded sympathetically, including the politicians present, but the defensive posture lacked the élan and sense of fair play that had characterized the earlier Carter. He was tired that night in the late fall of 1989, tired of the attacks or perceived attacks over episcopal negligence regarding clergy accused of sexual abuse, a negligence that entailed legal, fiscal and moral culpability. He was tired because he knew that he was largely powerless to arrest the damage being inflicted upon the Church, tired because he knew that he and his brother bishops were guilty of at least a negligence born of ignorance. And he was tired because no matter his personal history of professional interaction with the media, this time, things were different and he was leaving the national scene precisely at that moment when his leadership was most necessary. His combative stance was an act of desperation. Carter was too shrewd and self-knowing not to know that. He feared that "après moi le deluge" – the attacks would accelerate in volume and intensity. And they have.

Amid the onslaught of media exposés, investigations and revelations are to be found the more sustained insider accounts that purport to throw light on a dysfunctional institution hostile to reformation. Although Carter's 1989 public reprimand of an increasingly unfair and blindly partial media was categorical and defiant, he was not the first hierarch to bristle at the relentless media focus on clerical misdeeds; he was just the best known and most media savvy. But if Carter thought that his critique of unprofessional media coverage would somehow serve to stanch the bile – and he was too pragmatic and informed to believe that – he did think that his cry of outrage might have a mitigating effect on the growing multitude of shell-shocked Catholics. When it came to assessing credibility, Carter could see that even faithful Catholics were increasingly relying on the Church's critics and not the Church's princes to tell the truth. After all, scandals were arising throughout the Canadian landscape: Newfoundland – the Archdiocese of St. John's and the Mount Cashel Boys Home; accusations of abuse against Oblates of Mary Immaculate in the prairies; court cases concerning Christian Brother Training Schools in Alfred and Uxbridge, Ontario; charges of abuse by diocesan priests across the country, including Carter's former diocese of London.

Attention to the growing scandal of clerical sex abuse was not limited to reporters and columnists driven by editorial urgency or to broadcasters with a keen eye for the most shaming sound bite. Books would soon begin to appear that were not, on the surface, motivated by a desire to unearth yet greater infamies, but had about them an air of melancholy mixed with liberation. In other words, they were not conceived as broadsides but as personalized accounts, driven not by animus but by a therapeutic and spiritual need for closure. One of the best of this genre was T.F. Rigelhof's *A Blue Boy in a Black Dress* (1995). A gem of a work – gently evocative, unfinished, a recovered memory tentatively embraced – Rigelhof's Proustian experiment nudged an unaware or frightened Catholic readership in a new and necessary direction. Shortlisted for the Governor General's Award in non-fiction, the book resurfaced nine years later as both a much augmented thing and yet as something much less: *Nothing Sacred: A Journey Beyond Belief.*

Begun in the shadow of Cardinal Bernard Law's resignation as Archbishop of Boston in December 2002, and savagely interrupted by a stroke that brought the author close to death, *Nothing Sacred* "contains much more of the child who is father to this man than the format of the earlier book [*A Blue Boy*] permitted." The reader gets an unnerving foretaste of the latest iteration when Rigelhof explains in his Introduction, "For me, being reasonable means accepting human diversity and embracing it in all its messiness. Those who follow ideologues, including the oligarch in the white dress and the triple crown, with his court in Rome, will find my reasoning profoundly disordered."

It is not, of course, his attachment to reason that is problematic. It is rather his attachment to old-fashioned bigotry. And it is not just the Roman pontiff who comes in for a drubbing – after all, he has had centuries of such vituperation – but the Society of Jesus as well. It appears that Jesuits have "advanced training in psychological persecution and spiritual torment" and understand something of the first rule of terrorists: "keep your victim off balance." In a way it is understandable – Rigelhof's rhetoric of abuse – given that he was fondled and propositioned by one of the Jesuits when he was a lad at Campion High School in Regina, Saskatchewan. But is it "reasonable" to categorize all Jesuits as he does?

Rigelhof's swan song to Catholicism is heavily lacquered in its own exalted self-regard, feeds off its anger, and in the end becomes hysterical rather than historical. And this is unfortunate on several fronts. *A Blue Boy in a Black Dress* morphed from a curious memoir into an acidic apologia. From his plaintive evocation of a young boy's growth into manhood, attraction to a life of priestly witness, and struggle to know himself – psychologically and spiritually – *A Blue Boy in a Black Dress* provides valuable insight into the world of the minor seminary, clerical rigidity, adolescent self-doubt, the corrosive effects of mismanaged authority, and the destructive consequences of a false romanticism. It is an exquisitely crafted volume. But then it became *Nothing Sacred*.

The writings of disaffected Catholics, whether conceived out of anguish or with an eye to the opportune or both, deserve to be read, but specious claims to objectivity should be ruthlessly scrutinized. Memoirs, tracts, investigations and potboilers emerging out of the heart of the sex abuse maelstrom must be taken seriously: the fodder is rich and fertile. But not at the expense of rigorous diligence. Truth and justice cannot be sacrificed at the altar of self-aggrandizement and imaginative license.

The Canadian Jesuits, for instance, were especially proactive in addressing cases involving members of the order. Conscious of the need for effective enculturation, for a credible ministry to the Aboriginal peoples of Canada, and aware of their own historic importance as the Black Robes of the seventeenth century, the Upper Canada Province of the Society of Jesus built the Anishinabe Spiritual Centre on Anderson Lake in northern Ontario in 1980 with the express purpose of strengthening native leadership and healing the community in relation to all forms of addiction and dysfunction. Workshops, retreats, courses in theology and spirituality, and sessions for alcoholics and adult children of alcoholics were all designed to contribute to the building up rather than the eradication of the unique Aboriginal cultures that constitute an undervalued component of the Canadian fabric. The work of the Centre – incarnating or impregnating a culture with Christian values and spirituality in such a way that they do not distort or eliminate indigenous truths and customs – was best articulated by the late George Leach. As a result of both his scholarship and his close pastoral involvement at the Anishinabe Centre, Leach concluded that

> the work of the Centre was begun as the *continuation* of Jean de Brébeuf's dream, which is enfleshed in the letters that he wrote back to France in the 1640s, wherein he said that he hoped the Jesuits would develop a native clergy and that they in turn would run their own church. In addition, the work of the Centre involves an act of reparation, incorporating healing ceremonies; we have also had services on some of the different reserves at which time we have tried to surface some of the pain. At one elders conference on Birch Island at Dreamer's Rock, with everybody present, I just very simply said that: "on behalf of my Jesuit brothers of history I am sorry for what happened; I don't want to continue to look in the rearview window of the car; I need to say to you that I am sorry; I hope that I have not offended you; and I hope that we can work together to create a new future. Both human and divine."

The years of cultural insensitivity and denigration during which the Jesuits were both individually and collectively complicit, either because of historical biases and societal ignorance, or because of personal disorder (emotionally, sexually and physically abusive behaviour), needed to be acknowledged so that the good could shine unclouded by the sinister, the heroic service of the many undiminished by the evil of the few.

It is precisely because the Canadian Jesuits were resolved to understand the Aboriginal peoples that they established the Centre and started on their long road to mutual respect and trust between the races and the traditions. It hasn't been easy.

In 1990, reports of the sexual abuse of native boys by George Epoch, a Jesuit who served the Chippewa community on Cape Croker, Ontario, began to surface. The Jesuits immediately set up a counselling program for the abused and their families, provided cash compensation for each valid claimant (as well as additional monies for therapy and education for the victims and their families), and issued a public apology to all the victims and to the community as a whole. As the then Provincial of the order, Eric Maclean, said in his "homily/statement" at Cape Croker on August 30, 1992,

> I speak to you today as the Provincial Superior of the Canadian Jesuits … I come here in sorrow, in regret and in humility, acknowledging the wrong that the late Father Epoch [who died in 1986] did to you, expressing my sorrow and apologizing on my own behalf and that of all Canadian Jesuits for his actions and for the devastating consequences those actions have had in your lives and in the lives of your family and community … I ask you to allow us to work side by side, Native People and Jesuits. Along this pathway I hope and pray that we may continue, as in the past, to trust and respect each other as together we approach a challenging future.

Although most parties reached a financial and reconciliation agreement in 1994, the aftermath has been lingering, festering and damaging. Repairing the breach of trust symbolized by Epoch's disabling pedophilia is proving to be a long-term undertaking. Perhaps generational.

But the Canadian Jesuits addressed the issue with alacrity uncharacteristic of many orders and religious communities at the time. In many ways they were ahead of the game. In *Nothing Sacred*, T.F. Rigelhof cuts them no slack, however. He draws on caricatures and stereotypes of the Jesuits that would bring a blush to the cheek of the most ardent anti-Romish Elizabethan zealot.

The real object of his loathing is not the Society of Jesus; it is the Roman Catholic Church, as embodied in the papacy, an institution itself notoriously served by the Jesuits. Rigelhof's abhorrence of Catholic teaching on sexuality is really the point. His detestation of authoritarianism and Manichaeism is well placed, if seriously compromised by the excesses and emotionalism of his arguments. Many Catholics in good standing share Rigelhof's concerns about Catholic teaching on sexuality, but they avoid easy judgment. Instead, they look at the teaching in the context of history and conflicting models and systems of understanding, value the organic integrity of the teaching, appreciate the nuances involved in the teaching per se, and recognize the complexities of transmitting the teaching to an indifferent or uncomprehending generation.

Not all self-declared non-practising Catholic writers harbour resentment towards the Church or are motivated to exact revenge for injuries real or imagined. Some, like the 2009 Giller Award winner Linden MacIntyre, bring their literary talent to the formidable task of exploring with a hard sympathy the pathologies of ecclesiastical life without venting their spleen. He does not tread lightly when it comes to exposing evil, but he does so in a way that respects the contradictions, ambiguities and conflictive tensions that constitute individual as well as institutional life.

MacIntrye is a seasoned radio and television host/investigator with an impressive body of work. Himself the product of deeply Catholic Cape Breton Island, Nova Scotia, MacIntyre's novel *The Bishop's Man* has as its protagonist the very able but spiritually and emotionally troubled priest Duncan MacAskill, a reflective trouble-shooter for the bishop of his diocese. That diocese is Antigonish – pre–Raymond Lahey.

MacAskill is not personally implicated in any wrong-doing – he is, in fact, such a sturdy and professional cleric that the bishop relies on him to exercise a moral and legal surveillance over clerics with a questionable and sensitive history. In other words, it is up to MacAskill to keep those who hover on the threshold of moral misbehaviour and criminal conduct within constraints. The reputation of the Church must remain paramount.

MacAskill, unlike his superior, has a deep apprecia-tion of the "vipers' tangle" that is the human heart. He struggles regularly to understand what drives him per-sonally as a man, fights (largely unsuccessfully) with his own demons, and wrestles with his own isolation within the larger isolation:

> It was dark when I left. I could have spent the night at Holy Name or Holy Redeemer or St. Anthony Daniel. Any one of half a dozen parishes with their rambling, empty houses. But I knew what my unan-nounced arrival had come to mean. I knew what my

fellow priests would think, seeing me at the door. I could imagine the fleeting look of fear, then wariness. And then the long evening of formality. Or perhaps, after a drink or two, lectures on the wickedness of lay people and the anticlericalism that was surfacing and victimizing all of us. How we should all be covering each other's backs, not making matters worse, feeding the flames of hysteria.

The defensive posture adopted by many of the clergy – understandable when, as a group, they see themselves under perpetual siege – is not, however, the predominant response of most in the priesthood. It is far more likely to be an unhealthy brew of feelings including shame, contrition, puzzlement, anger at fraternal betrayal, abandonment at the hands of a frightened hierarchy, and incomprehension in the face of rising public hostility to an office once respected unlike any other.

The novel happened to be published in 2009, the same year Raymond Lahey was arrested. MacIntyre noted in an article for *The Globe and Mail* that the front-line workers – the priests, nuns and deacons of the Diocese of Antigonish – "will have to manage the fallout from this catastrophe. For, regardless of the outcome of the courts of law, there has already been a verdict in the court of public opinion." He had a major precedent for how this would unfold in the Mount Cashel and St. John's pastoral and ethical meltdown in Newfoundland in the 1980s and 1990s. And there are several parallels and connections between the two jurisdictions.

Mount Cashel Orphanage for boys – the inception of which dates back to the late nineteenth century – was under the direction of the Christian Brothers of Ireland for the last forty years of its existence. In 1975, the Royal Newfoundland Constabulary launched a criminal investigation to follow up on allegations of sexual and physical abuse at the orphanage. The investigation was truncated and resulted in the removal of two staff members, who were then placed in rehabilitation centres outside of Newfoundland. In 1982, a second investigation was conducted and one Irish Christian Brother was convicted.

But matters were not brought to closure. In 1989, a flood of media revelations forced the reopening of the prematurely curtailed 1975 investigation. Michael Harris, publisher of the province's weekly newspaper *The Sunday Express*, began to publish allegations of abuse dating back to the 1950s (he would later write the major study of the Mount Cashel cover-up – *Unholy Orders: Tragedy at Mount Cashel*); the province established the Hughes Royal Commission to explore the obstruction of justice; Shane Earle, one of the most vocal and passionate victim's of abuse, launched a civil lawsuit against both the Government of Newfoundland and Labrador and the Archdiocese of St. John's; and the Archbishop of St. John's appointed his own commission of inquiry known as the Winter Commission. The national spotlight was on Newfoundland. When the Winter Commission published its report in 1990 (the Hughes Commission would appear in 1992), at least one head would roll.

The sight was both pathetic and noble. There on the most important public affairs television program of the Canadian Broadcasting Corporation – *The Journal* – was Alphonsus Penney, Archbishop of St John's, publicly acknowledging his pastoral failure over the vexatious issue of clerical pedophilia and the institutional Church's lamentable and wholly inadequate response to the complaints of victims. It was an indictment complete and entire; it was an act of repentance on the part of a culpable but honourable prelate quite simply overtaken by the enormity of it all. Earlier on that fateful day, July 18, 1990, he had proffered his resignation as archbishop.

At the press conference convened on his own authority, Penney remarked,

> I apologize and express my sincere regrets for failing the victims and their families in their moment of acute pain and desolation. I also express to the people of God in our local Church my regrets for the deficiency in leadership, ministry and management. I take full responsibility and candidly acknowledge that "it is I the shepherd", indeed the chief shepherd, who has failed. Upon becoming aware of the significantly negative evaluation of my leadership, ministry and management, I immediately wrote our Holy Father, Pope John Paul II, and submitted my resignation as Archbishop of St John's.

The "negative evaluation" of his pastorship to which he alluded was expressed in particular in the report on child sexual abuse by members of the clergy of Newfoundland. This report was drawn up by the archdiocesan commission of inquiry, widely known as the Winter Commission after its chairman, Gordon Winter, a former Lieutenant Governor and an Anglican. Ironically, Penney himself established the commission and set its mandate. Although it clearly intended to respond to the mounting criticism of the archbishop's performance, and was a constructive effort to assure the Catholic community of Newfoundland of the chief shepherd's determination not to play down the gravity of the issue, Penney could not have anticipated the harsh verdict that his leadership would be accorded. The two-volume report's 55 conclusions and recommendations were hard-hitting.

The Church of Newfoundland had been under severe public scrutiny. The series of sex scandals involving altar boys and orphans had shaken the Catholic community in the province to its very roots. In the major newspapers of the nation, principally in *The Globe and Mail* and the *Toronto Star*, as well as in such national news magazines as *L'Actualité* and *Maclean's*, detailed coverage had been provided on a regular basis. Weekly, or even daily, installments about the behaviour of the Newfoundland clergy provoked rage, indignation or titillation.

It began with the trial of Fr. James Hickey, one of the most popular priests in all of Atlantic Canada. It was Hickey who figured prominently as a master planner during the first papal visit to Canada in 1984, and it was Hickey who could be relied upon to employ his native charm to stunning effect with the media. This same Hickey was found guilty of a score of sexual assaults upon altar boys spanning several years, and was sentenced to five years in prison, to be served at the Dorchester penitentiary in New Brunswick. He was repeatedly denied early parole and died in prison.

During the Hickey trial, other allegations concerning priests and ex-priests surfaced, fanning the flames of outrage, embarrassment and confusion. Penney chose silence as his legal and moral strategy. He was counselled to do so. It may have proven to be legally wise, although this is doubtful, but morally his leadership suffered irreparable damage. He only became truly apprised of the extent of the damage upon receiving the Winter Commission's report. After an anxious laity met the initial disclosures with shock and incredulity, Penney found himself increasingly targeted by angry Catholics for his "policy" of inaction, a form of pastoral solicitude they could easily do without. There were calls for his resignation. He declined to visit the parishes whose resident priests stood accused or were facing charges – frequently dispatching the articulate and affable Fr. Kevin Molloy in his stead – and avoided the media completely.

As a result, Penney's credibility and that of many of his clergy plummeted in the public eye. The clerical authority was replaced by a highly credible moral authority invested in several women religious and in an increasingly vocal laity, composed of many activist mothers and aggrieved parents. In a manner consonant with the method of liberation theology, these unofficial spokeswomen have provided a cogent dissection of the pathology of patriarchy and a painful analysis of the dangers of a rampant clericalism.

As if these disclosures were not enough, the headlines were soon taken over by allegations of sexual and physical abuse made against several Irish Christian Brothers by past residents of Mount Cashel Orphanage in St. John's. These charges, and the accusations of a cover-up perpetrated by a Church-State alliance of feudal proportions, led to the creation of the Hughes Commission and the closure of Mount Cashel.

Religious controversy and religious shenanigans are not new to Catholics in Canada's youngest province. But the shame and seediness associated with pedophilia and pederasty have eroded, irreversibly, the exaggerated esteem the clergy commanded, particularly in the outport villages along the coast.

Not a few of the priests and scores of the religious sisters were comforted by that knowledge at least. Clericalism is dying in Newfoundland – a region more devoutly and fiercely Catholic than almost anywhere else in Canada, including the pockets of Acadian and Celtic Catholicism found in the Maritimes or the immigrant communities of Toronto and Montreal.

The nasty drama that unfolded in the province prompted the editor of *Saturday Night* magazine to observe in the January/February 1990 issue,

> From the Church in Canada recently we have been learning more than we ever wanted to know about the dark side of trust. This has to be corrected in a forthright, public manner, no matter how painful the process is. And it will be painful because reforms in the public sector are caught up with all those thorny family matters that have to be struggled with urgently and alone.

Those "thorny family matters" were struggled with in stark relief against the backdrop of the Winter Commission and an archbishop's resignation. Many of the Commission's recommendations were predictable, but many others were blunt assessments of inadequate and morally, if not criminally, culpable actions on the part of the Church leadership. The archdiocesan administration was urged to accept its full share of guilt and responsibility, indulging in no waffling or evasionary tactics, recognizing the vulnerability of the victims and seeking in every public way to provide compensation and healing. But what is especially surprising is the Commission's strong insistence that the Canadian Conference of Catholic Bishops undertake broader initiatives to develop a "national program of research and study which might contribute to the development of the Church's theology of sexuality." In addition, the Commission boldly recommended that Penney and his episcopal brothers across Canada address "fully, directly, honestly and without reservation questions relating to the problematic link between celibacy and the ministerial priesthood."

The first major occasion for the bishops to respond to this recommendation came with their plenary assembly in August, just a few weeks after the release of the Winter Commission's report. They set aside part of their time to address, yet again, the problem of sex abuse, but hesitated to do more. They had their own committee, a committee that would produce a groundbreaking document two years later, a committee charged with the mandate to examine the issue with all its ramifications. The bishops also demonstrated their willingness to establish diocesan procedures to cope with complaints and the need to guarantee due process of law. There were other urgent items, however, they reasoned, that required attention, and the sex scandals had sapped the energy of an already overextended and demoralized clergy. But the bishops missed an ideal moment. As they mulled over their drafts of the interventions [brief addresses, approximately three minutes long, designed to articulate the position of the episcopal conference or assembly that the bishop who is speaking represents] for the Synod in Rome that October of 1990 – refining, clarifying and tightening the wording – they chose *not* to address any of the clerical abuse controversies roiling unabated in Canada, nor to call for serious structural change regarding the priesthood, innovative amendments to priestly formation, or any change to the discipline of celibacy.

The history of Canadian synodal interventions is a heroic one. Canada's bishops have raised questions other episcopal conferences have either not contemplated or have not dared to express in public. It was the 1971 intervention of Cardinal Flahiff, for instance, that first took up the issue of women and ministry, to which the CCCB returned with tenacity and creativity at the Synods in 1980, 1983, 1985 and 1987.

Pope John Paul II, however, made it clear that he did not want a discussion of clerical celibacy at the 1990 Synod on the training of priests. An intervention specifically focused on celibacy could therefore be seen as rank insubordination. However, given the problems facing the ministerial priesthood in Canada – an increasing number of priestless parishes, particularly in the prairie provinces; a high burnout rate among active clergy; flourishing rehabilitative services for clergy; an average clerical age hovering around the late 60s; starkly inadequate seminary enrollments; and so on – it is hard to justify the exclusion of the subject from the interventions. Temerity, not timidity, is what Canadian Catholics wanted from their bishops at the time.

Three of the five delegates – Aloysius Ambrozic of Toronto, Frederick Henry of London, and Henri Goudreault of Labrador-Schefferville – were former seminary professors or rectors, so it was not unreasonable to expect of them interventions of an immediate and pointed nature. Such had been the tradition of the past.

This time, however, prudence displaced candour. The interventions failed to examine alternatives to seminary education or new models of priestly ministry. Given the highly charged atmosphere in Canada over the sex abuse scandal, and the continued failure of recruitment programs to attract a significant number of high-quality candidates for the priesthood, what could possibly have motivated the bishops to choose so tame and tepid an approach, if not an ingrained awareness that anything that departed from the pope's express will – what topics to exclude or avoid – would be perceived as disloyal and counterproductive on their part?

The events in Newfoundland – trials, judicial inquiries and committee reports – easily obscured the need for a more accurate historical and ecclesial evaluation of the accountability of the hierarchy, the training of Church personnel, fair financial compensation for victims of clerical crime, sexual and emotional rehabilitation, and the subsequent reintegration into the service of Church of those who underwent restorative therapy.

The forming of a Coalition of Concerned Canadian Catholics, and the increasing boldness with which various lay Catholics demanded accountability from those who exercised Church office, were signs of the times. Though Canadian Catholics are not restive or rebellious by nature – after all, Canada retains historical and political links with the British Crown – the sex abuse scandals in Newfoundland brought to a head Catholics' many worries about whether those who govern the Church have the capacity on their own to effect deep and authentic structural change.

The first step out of the Newfoundland maelstrom had been taken with the Winter Commission's report showing the way to turn tragedy into the beginning of wisdom. But as stated earlier, the Canadian bishops had been far from inactive during the period of the Winter and Hughes Commissions. In fact, as early as October of 1989 they had established their ad hoc committee on child sexual abuse.

The committee produced a collection of materials for discussion called "Breach of Trust, Breach of Faith" and published its report, *From Pain to Hope*, in June 1992. Both documents were significant and estimable efforts showing an honesty and determination even the Church's critics admired. But it was not the end of the crisis. The Church had lost a great deal of credibility over the years due to these scandals and the suspicion that there were attempts to conceal these intolerable acts.

The committee was chaired by Archbishop Roger Ébacher of Gatineau-Hull and was composed of two other archbishops (Adam Exner, OMI, and James Mac-Donald, CSC), a lay social worker (André Boyer), a social development officer (Rita Cadieux), the national president of the Councils of Priests (Gerard Copeman), and a Sister of Charity who is a pediatrician and bioethicist (Nuala Kenny). It had four specialist assistants: Frank Morrisey, OMI, former Dean of the Faculty of Canon Law at Saint Paul University in Ottawa; Paul McAuliffe, a social worker; Jacques Gagné, professor of pastoral counselling and past rector of the Saint Paul University Seminary; and Jeannine Guindon, a psychotherapist. Some 25 collaborators drawn from medicine, civil and canon law, social work, nursing, theology, psychiatry and psychology rounded out the committee.

From Pain to Hope contained 50 recommendations, many of them bold, all of them urgent. The report was neither timid nor delicate in acknowledging the abuse that had flourished without accountability. It even looked at the priesthood in Canada in order to detect signs of institutional pathology that go beyond the simple recording of personal sexual disorder and occasional aberration.

The committee noted that "relatively recently in our history, Catholic priests in Canada could, on account of their ministry and their status as priests, exercise considerable authority over the day-to-day lives of their communities." This "excessive power," it declares,

> unchecked by any kind of social control, placed certain individuals beyond the reach of legitimate questioning and made it possible to prevent detection. The fact that priests were placed on a pedestal was actually a kind of trap. This contributed to their becoming more and more isolated from the people they serve and not developing healthy relationships built on simple friendship – something essential to a balanced humanity.

The committee recommended that in the spirit of humility "more energy be put into correcting wrongs than into safeguarding appearances; into humble care of the wounded than into attempts to justify; into effective forms of education and careful research into ways of improving services for children, the poor and the most vulnerable in our society."

Those were the words of an institution that was contrite, wounded, moving "from pain to hope."

The first five recommendations were addressed to all the Catholics of Canada and vigorously encouraged the citizenry to become informed about every aspect – juridical, psychological and social – concerning sexual abuse of children and the demands of healing.

The report then addressed the Catholic bishops of Canada (recommendations 6 to 23), mostly on legal and procedural matters, including the process to be invoked should consideration be given to the possible return to active ministry of a priest who, having been convicted of child sexual abuse and having served his sentence or having received a suspended sentence, asked to resume his ministry. These recommendations came under some heavy criticism. Many parishes in the country are still smarting from ill-advised shuffles in the past, when abusive priests were simply reassigned to a different parish or transferred to a different diocese without the new congregation or bishop being made fully aware of the priest's record. The report, however, made clear that the priest who is to be reintegrated "should be prepared to meet with the members of the parish council or with a group of parishioners to ask for their support, understanding and prayer."

The hard investigative work in exposing these abuses was done, particularly in the early days, by the secular media. John Redekop, a political science professor and a columnist for the Evangelical and Reformed newspaper *Christian Week*, rightly pointed out that the defensive posture adopted by the fundamentalist media in the United States over the televangelist sex scandals of the

1980s (Jimmy Swaggart and Jim Bakker) was matched in Canada with an alarming timidity among the religious over the Roman Catholic clerical sexual abuse scandal. In fact, when *Catholic New Times* of Toronto republished a news item from a Calgary newspaper concerning sexual assault allegations against a British Columbia bishop, the Oblate Bishop of Prince George, Hubert O'Connor, the editors were inundated with complaints, cancellations of subscriptions, and more than a mite of outrage. The rumours, however, were translated into formal charges and the bishop resigned, admitted to consensual sex with at least two women, and was jailed for sexual assault.

Perhaps an awareness of the consequences of damage control was behind the committee's clear call for openness:

> ... our suggestions and recommendations are clearly oriented towards the search for truth: the truthfulness of statements made to the media; personal truthfulness and honesty on the preparation of candidates for the priesthood; insistence on the truth throughout the therapy of the abusers; truthfulness with those few parishes asked to accept a priest who is being reintegrated into the ministry.

This approach is meant to exorcise the demon of secrecy, the fear of causing scandal. Yet, as Andrew Britz, the blunt-speaking Benedictine editor of *The Prairie Messenger*, noted,

> The report calls on Catholics to "break the silence" about child sexual abuse, but is itself silent about the magnitude of the problem. When reporters asked for figures on the number of cases involving child sexual

abuse by priests and religious, the committee was unable to do as much as hazard a guess. Yet an Ottawa newspaper was later able to come up with a list of 70 priests and members of religious orders who have been charged with sexual offences in recent years.

The committee failed to understand that *modified* openness is not openness at all.

Another set of recommendations (24 to 33) was addressed to those responsible for priestly formation. In an accompanying preliminary note, the authors remarked that these recommendations were not "intended to replace the orientation document of the Holy See in 1980." It was discreet to say so, but in so doing the committee revealed the considerable difficulty it faced when addressing national issues in a universal institution. The recommendations argued for the formation of seminarians "within a context of integral human development" and relied rather heavily on the insights and methods of the social sciences. They did not jettison the philosophical and theological curricula so dear to the heart of Rome, but they did support such things as human formation counsellors and made a point of emphasizing "how necessary it is that women be among those who collaborate in the formation of candidates for the priesthood. The involvement of women is considered essential at all stages and every aspect of the formation (including teaching, counseling and pastoral work)."

The presence of Dr. Jeannine Guindon as one of the four principal advisers to the committee was instructive. A professional psychotherapist, she was invited by Pope John Paul II to attend the 1990 Synod on priestly formation as a lay auditor. Her presence might well have emboldened the committee to press some of these matters of priestly training that Rome continues to be suspicious of – such as the enhanced presence of women in priestly formation.

To those responsible for priests in a diocese, the committee proposed various ways of diminishing clerical isolation and loneliness and of enhancing opportunities for mutual support. The last seven recommendations of the report addressed the bishops' conference itself, encouraging it in its role as facilitator and urging the creation and implementation of a code of professional ethics for clergy and pastoral agents.

The bishops of Canada had the daunting task of implementing the recommendations made by their ad hoc committee. Although the report did not employ a hard ecclesiological critique of the inadequacies of Church structure and formation, it did admit to the presence of such serious problems as "the failure to fully implement ecclesial communion proposed by the Second Vatican Council," and the committee's working papers, "Breach of Trust, Breach of Faith," did include several passages from the Winter Commission. This one outlines the ravages of patriarchy:

> Paternalism and sexism are very much in evidence, the commission was told, among both young and old priests in the archdiocese. Many who spoke and presented briefs to the commission described an alarming lack of awareness and insensitivity in the use of patriarchal language and imagery in worship, and in preaching and teaching throughout the archdiocese ... Many have argued that patriarchal thinking is one of the contributing factors to the sexual abuse of

children. This brave inclusion is, however, provided with an italicized note indicating that "the quotations pertaining to each factor are discussion starters only. Debate and further study of these complex matters are needed and encouraged."

But the report of the bishops' ad hoc committee – *From Pain to Hope* – was limited to the issue of child sexual abuse. Crimes of sexual assault, allegations of sexual impropriety and harassment regarding those aged 18 and older of either sex, and the highly vexatious issue of abuse in the native residential schools fell outside its mandate. However, the sexual abuse incidents in St. John's and St. Joseph's training schools, run by the Christian Brothers in Ontario, did fall within the mandate. The committee's work was applauded by David McCann, the founder of Helpline (a support group for survivors of physical and sexual abuse) and a major force in creating awareness of the appalling legacy of abuse.

At the time the CCCB's report was published, the Roman Catholic Church was not the only church facing major challenges to its institutional integrity on matters of sexual injustice. Revelations about the Mennonite community in the prairie provinces, the highly publicized trials of two Anglican choirmasters in Toronto and Kingston, and a report on sexual abuse by the clergy of the United Church of Canada demonstrated only too clearly that the Catholic Church was not alone in its painful exercise in self-scrutiny. In fact, it was a national leader in coping with the challenges and fallout of clerical sexual abuse among faith communities in Canada and a model for the global Catholic Church. The report's summary and conclusion are masterful examples of enlightened and honest critique. They diagnose the complex factors involved, eschew categorical judgment, and face the systemic issues – social and ecclesiastical – with matchless forthrightness:

> At the beginning of the sixth part of our report, we expressed the firm conviction that the concerted effort of many people will be needed to stem the tide of sexual abuse against children. To conclude this section, let us state where the Catholic Church should stand in the context of this plan for action.
>
> - On the side of openness and truth: We would like to see our church guided by a spirit of openness and truth when responding to allegations of child sexual abuse by a priest or a religious. We want our church to cooperate fully with child-protection agencies and the judiciary, not claiming preferential treatment for one of its ministers when suspected or formally accused in such cases.
>
> - On the side of extensive cooperation by Catholics: In our minds, our church would be socially irresponsible if it participated in the fight against child sexual abuse only when one of its ministers is implicated. We know that such cases represent only a small proportion of the total number of cases in our country.
>
> We would like to see our church, inspired equally by belief in the cause itself and by a sense of responsibility, actively encourage all Catholics to cooperate fully with Health and Welfare Canada in its efforts to curb family violence and, in particular, child sexual abuse. Our church should call its members to unite with those who condemn such forms of aggression.

- On the side of transforming persons and institutions: We would like to see our church face, with clarity and courage, the decisions that must be taken in light of the failure that child abuse represents for society and the church itself. Indeed, it is simply intolerable that a society should degenerate to the extent of closing its eyes to the injustices which are destroying the foundations on which children build their identity.

These decisions will call for change in the attitudes of those who are whole-heartedly to defend children and other vulnerable people in society. They also call for change in institutions themselves, both those in civil society and those within the church.

Child sexual abuse flourishes in a society that is based on competition and power and which is undermined by sexual exploitation and violence against women. Contemporary society has shown itself quick to reject traditional values, to be unable to offer new ones and to be unfair to women and children. The challenge to transform society becomes enormous when we begin to realize the terrible social cost when child abuse is tolerated.

Another contributing factor to child sexual abuse is a church that too readily shelters its ministers from having to account for their conduct; that is often tempted to settle moral problems behind a veil of secrecy, which only encourages their growth; that has not yet fully developed a process on internal reform in which the values of familial communion would predominate. Challenges for personal conversion and institutional change are far from lacking. We would like to see our church take firm steps which would leave no doubt as to its genuine desire to eradicate the phenomenon of child sexual abuse.

The two years of study we undertook in response to the request of the Canadian Conference of Catholic Bishops have taught us a great deal about the insidious character of sexual abuse. Within limits of our studies, our discussions and the reports of our work groups, we have been able to come to a better understanding of the extent of the devastation caused by this abuse. The devastation touches the whole community to one degree or another: the families and friends of the victims; those in their immediate community (school, neighborhood, parish, Scout troop, sports club, activities center, etc.); and the groups linked to the abusers (teaching staff, medical institutions, clergy, psychologists and the psychiatrists, therapists, etc.). In varying degrees, these persons or agencies were obliged to live in an atmosphere of mistrust, suspicion, insidious accusation and at times contempt.

The path of humility is no less important. Even if only a tiny fraction of Canada's 11,000 priests in active ministry have been implicated in cases of abuse, the church must humbly admit that some of its ministers are in flagrant contradiction to the message they have been commissioned to preach.

Knowing well that we have not said the final word in response to these difficult questions, with humility we ask our readers: "Are we right in believing that we, as church can pass from pain to hope?"

Since the publication of this universally applauded document – episcopal conferences outside of Canada and indeed the Vatican itself have benefited from this pioneering work – numerous other cases of sexual abuse by Canadian clergy have arisen, testing the insights, feasibility, institutional will, episcopal resolve, financial resources, legal flexibility and ecclesiastical priorities of dioceses and religious orders and congregations across the nation. Trials, litigations, settlements and prison sentences have commanded relentless media attention, redirected institutional energies away from other pressing pastoral priorities, and drained the spirit and morale of countless numbers of clerics and laypeople.

Charles Sylvestre and Barry Glendinning of the Diocese of London, Ontario; Bernard Prince of the Diocese of Pembroke, Ontario (also a dicasterial honorary prelate working in Rome for decades); Allan A. MacDonald of the Diocese of Antigonish, Nova Scotia: these are just a few of the names of investigated, judged, sentenced and, in some cases, formally defrocked clerics. There are many others.

Their number is not wildly disproportionate to cases found in other professions; the media coverage, however, is.

And if this is true of the emotional, sexual and physical abuse perpetrated by clerics and religious brothers and sisters in dioceses, training schools and orphanages, it is especially true – given the political and cultural undercurrents – of the Residential Schools crisis that has roiled Canada for the past two decades. The Anglican and United Churches participated in running and supervising residential schools for Aboriginal children across Canada at the same time as the Roman Catholic Church. These churches were all charged to do so by the federal government and its appropriate ministries; before the closure of these schools, they functioned as places where the languages, customs, and indigenous religious traditions of the Aboriginal peoples were methodically eliminated. These church-operated residential schools – and they were commissioned by the federal authorities to do so – followed a methodology that is now generally considered a form of "cultural genocide." The schools no longer exist, regional compensation settlements have been negotiated, all the partners responsible for the operation of the residential schools have accepted their fiscal and ethical obligations (although this proved a much longer and tortuously contorted route for the Catholic Church, because of its unique canonical structure – it is not a national church in the same way that the Anglican and United Churches are), and a national Truth and Reconciliation Commission, embroiled in its own political controversies at its formal inception, has been put in place to bring to a formal end a tragic, misguided and painful chapter in the nation's history. (This issue will be discussed at greater length in Chapter Seven.)

It is not as if the Canadian Church has been paralyzed by the revelations, media clamour and deepening ecclesial disquiet around the scandals, however. There are outstanding instances of episcopal initiative, personal courage and demonstrative pastoral leadership.

Bishop Ronald Fabbro of London, Ontario, a professionally trained ethicist and former Superior General of the Congregation of Saint Basil, dealt with the ugly aftermath of Father Charles Sylvestre's abuse of 47 girls between 1954 and 1990. Fabbro met with the victims personally; formed a diocesan sexual abuse committee; held workshops for the clergy and the laity of the diocese that included among their facilitators a University of Western Ontario psychologist as well as the victims themselves; drew up a code of conduct for priests; created a formal support network for the victims; and delivered a homily in 2006 at the Church of St. Ursula, Chatham, that incorporated an apology of sharp remorse and genuine contrition that acknowledged publicly the abuse the victims "endured at the hands of Father Sylvestre" and the "failure of the church to protect the victims and their families."

In addition, Fabbro wrote the prologue to a book by Paul Baily, the crown attorney involved in the proceedings – *From Isolation to Action: Child Sexual Abuse by Clergy* (2008) – underscoring his own commitment to ending the "scourge" of abuse.

Bishops Paul-André Durocher of Alexandria-Cornwall, Ontario, Gerald Wiesner, OMI, of Prince George, and Douglas Crosby, OMI, the new bishop of Hamilton, and former bishop of Corner Brook and Labrador (including what used to be the Diocese of St. George's) have worked assiduously and transparently to heal the wounds of the dioceses they inherited as Ordinaries. To create trust, credibility and forthright protocols of interaction among all the parties involved in a clerical abuse case – the perpetrator, the victims, the civil and ecclesiastical authorities, and the broader Catholic parish community – is no mean feat.

The Oblate bishop Douglas Crosby, in particular, achieved a staggering success in a climate of almost total collapse while in charge of St. George's. In order to compensate the three dozen victims of Father Kevin Bennett (he abused altar boys over the period spanning

1961 to 1989 and served four years in prison), Crosby required the diocese to sell its various properties to meet its obligations, launched lawsuits against insurance carriers that refused to cover compensation, undertook numerous public spiritual exercises in reparation and renewal, made appeals across the nation for moral and financial assistance, and faced the challenges of a demoralized clergy and scandalized laity with authentic pastoral humility and candour.

Elsewhere, Aloysius Ambrozic, while Cardinal Archbishop of Toronto, instituted the toughest sex abuse policy in the country, and perhaps, at the time, in the universal Church. It had about it a one-strike-and-you're-out rigour and categorical thoroughness.

But it is the media coverage that defines the parameters in which the story is told and shaped.

The most compelling question then becomes this: Who are the narrative shapers and how do they work?

3

A World in Flames

In the fall of 2009, the gnomic, combative and feisty television critic for *The Globe and Mail*, John Doyle, observed of the scandal swirling around disgraced late-night television host David Letterman (a scandal involving disclosures around Mr. Letterman's insatiable libido) that sleeping with the staff is commonplace in the industry and that the host's on-air contrition – "I come from the Lutheran Midwest" – is far from persuasive. Indeed, Doyle writes with something of the fervour of a Savonarola:

> Careers are made or destroyed through sexual relations ... Male authority figures – producers, directors, network and studio execs – have a sense of entitlement about sex with women looking for work. It is accepted inside the business and rarely discussed outside of it. ... Sexual exploitation is so common that some showbiz types are puzzled that the rest of society finds it disgusting ... It's ridiculous to talk of Letterman being fired. Something far more dark

than what has emerged will have to be revealed before that's a possibility. It's redundant to talk about "damage control," as if Letterman were a politician needing to manipulate the news cycle.

It's time to talk about the casting couch and the exploitation of women in the TV and movie rackets. But it won't happen. Nobody wants to talk about it. It's not a joke and it's not isolated to one talk show, one network or one movie set. Too many women in the entertainment racket understand and accept the reality that they're there to service men. That won't change soon, but it should. (*The Globe and Mail*, Oct. 5, 2009)

The rampant disregard for equity, sexual propriety, and ethical behaviour in the entertainment workplace will not come as a shock to a celebrity-saturated culture that obsesses about every infidelity, sexual misadventure and sexual experimentation conceivable. After all, the number of magazines, websites and blogs given to the ponderous recording of every breath expended by the "stars" can ill afford to stand in judgment on that caste that feeds it. Titillation sells as well as *schadenfreude*.

Doyle knows that the culture needs changing and that there is little interest by the industry – or indeed in society at large – that would inspire reformers to think that such a change is achievable this side of eternity. And so, David Letterman will continue to amuse his vast audience, publicly repent of his disloyalty to his new wife, take steps to ensure that whistle blowing in the future has limited scope in the local shop, and begin the repair to his image. On the latter point, unlike the more hapless golf *wunderkind*, Tiger Woods, whose serial adulteries would bring a blush to the cheek of the heavily rouged Nero, Letterman appears to have skillfully handled his restoration with, if anything, an increase in viewers – some acolytes, some voyeurs, most bemused.

There was little in the way of moral outrage in the public at large. Some disappointment, for sure, and perhaps even a little surprise, but tough to find the outrage. After all, even though some sponsors might be nervous – with Woods they were hysterical – what happens in the world of entertainment is "special," for we must always make allowances for art.

Think Polanski!

Roman Polanski, the Polish-American filmmaker, artiste, septuagenarian and occasional provocateur was arrested on September 26, 2009, while attempting to cross into Switzerland with the intention of attending a film festival at which he was to be honoured. Known throughout the world as the director of such films as *Knife in the Water, Rosemary's Baby, Macbeth, Chinatown, The Tenant, The Pianist,* and *The Ghost,* he is also known as the husband of the brutally murdered actor Sharon Tate (butchered along with several others by the mass murderer Charles Manson in 1969) and as a fugitive from American justice in the case of one thirteen-year-old San Fernando Valley girl named Samantha Gailey.

Polanski drugged and raped Gailey at Jack Nicholson's home in March of 1977 and was indicted by a Los Angeles County grand jury on six felony charges, including rape by use of drugs and furnishing a controlled substance to a minor. Following a plea bargain that saw Polanski plead guilty to the least serious of the charges – unlawful sex with a minor (which is classified as statutory rape) – he fled to Europe on the eve of his sentencing – January 31, 1978 – and has remained there since.

Although Polanski's outlaw status has been known for some time, and although the American authorities were diligent in trying to get him back to the U.S. for sentencing, the world largely looked the other way. After all, the creator of great cinema, the traumatized spouse, the survivor of the Krakow ghetto and Nazi tyranny should be cut a little slack. At least, so mused his professional peers.

When he was arrested 32 years into his exile, the filmmakers, actors, writers and others throughout the world – mostly Europe, in fact – who rallied to his defense ignored the crime, celebrated the genius, and expected that the fuss was really the result of an anti-quated morality crusade orchestrated by the American Right. The names of petitioners who denounced Po-lanski's arrest and subsequent incarceration as simply "a case of morals" included such cinema luminaries as Steven Soderbergh, Neil Jordan, Sam Mendes and Mike Nichols, authors of such international calibre as Salman Rushdie and Milan Kundera (no strangers to persecution themselves), and various French politicians, including President Nicolas Sarkozy.

But, as writer Jeffrey Toobin has noted, the "anti-Polanski backlash" proved formidable, bringing together in an uncomfortable alliance figures from divergent moral and philosophical perspectives. They could nonetheless find common cause in their abhorrence of the legal ab-erration scandalously illustrated by the easy clemency being argued for the far from contrite Roman Polanski:

Columnists across the political spectrum, from feminists on the left to conservatives on the right, found common cause in revulsion at both Polanski and his famous friends. Martha Pollitt wrote in *The Nation*, "It's enraging that literary superstars who go on and on about human dignity, and human rights, and even women's rights (at least when the women are Muslim) either don't see what Polanski did as rape, or don't care, because he is, after all, Polanski – an artist like themselves." The *Wall Street Journal's* drama critic wrote, "Anyone who lives in a tightly sealed echo chamber of self-congratulation, surrounded by yes-men who are dedicated to doing what he wants is bound to lose touch with reality." ("The Celebrity Defense," *The New Yorker*, December 14, 2009)

The case for exceptionality, the openness for amnesty, the sense of artistic entitlement that make for the argument of the defense of Roman Polanski – his release on the grounds that his talent excuses him from the obligations and duties that govern most mortals – is a case that is at its best romantic and at its worst Nietzschean in origin. The result is the same: artists are a special breed to be accorded special consideration.

What is true of artists and stars like late-night television hosts is also true of sports heroes, even when their behaviour is far from heroic. And, by extension, the masters of the sports heroes: the coaches. In many ways, the coaches exercise more control over the careers and fortunes of their players than most spectators and enthusiasts are aware of, an influence that can extend from the playing field or ice rink to the bedroom.

Sports and crime columnist Christie Blatchford, writing about former NHL player Theo Fleury's revelation that he had been sexually abused as a teenager by his coach, succinctly tallies the cost:

> Most adult men who are kind to vulnerable boys are merely being kind, but predators can practically smell out those kids – the lonely boy, the fatherless one, the fat one, the shunned one. Mr. Fleury would have been ripe for the picking – his dad was an alcoholic, his mom flattened out by sedatives. They were unalert parents who thought Graham James was the best thing to happen to their boy … For people who have had their trust so egregiously betrayed, their youth so exploited, there is no single answer. But shifting the shame to the right shoulders, the blame to where it belongs, usually lightens the burden. (*The Globe and Mail*, October 17, 2009)

In all three of the above instances, all discrete in kind and genesis, there are some commonalities. Letterman, Polanski and James all abused to some degree their position of power. The nature of that abuse varies – clearly, Letterman's and Woods' were consensual and not criminal – and the consequences for their victims is proportionate to the gravity of the perpetrator's actions. But what is important to notice – in addition to the fact that sexual transgressions by the mighty and the powerful (no matter what the locus of that power) command immediate and obsessive media attention – is the fact that the public's revulsion versus its titillation is selective. There are sins one is permitted and there are sins that are *verboten*.

And there are people, more specifically a class of people, who are uniquely identified for swift and unrelenting opprobrium. That class is the Roman Catholic clergy. Not so much in relation to priestly affairs with women, the fathering of children with mistresses, the periodic dalliance and skewering of the chastity commitment. No. Rather, the predilection for boys, whether post- or pre-pubescent. And it all gets rather muddled.

Canadian contrarian and writer Margaret Wente, in a column on the Tiger Woods media and sponsorship furor around his numberless trysts (names of his lovers were emerging daily and with dizzying effect), opined that she had a lot of sympathy for the alpha male golfer because "after all, he's not a politician or a priest."

This throwaway comment encapsulates the public's cynicism towards errant politicians – the governors of New Jersey, New York and South Carolina come to mind – but also betrays the public's perception that Catholic priests are especially susceptible to hypocrisy and perversity. This perception is at the heart of much of the media coverage of the scandals: there is an increasingly low tolerance for white crime, political deception and image-manipulation, leadership foibles, and special privilege. The Catholic priesthood – either hysterically venerated, mercilessly spoofed and now shamelessly eviscerated – is especially vulnerable to media hype and cynicism.

There are reasons for that perception: the cumulative impact of pedophilia charges; the preponderance of negative images associated with priests; society's hypersensitivity when it comes to the security of its young; false memory syndrome; residential schools scandals; growing hostility towards an exclusively male authority figure; deep distrust of all religious authorities post-9/11; intolerance for any culture that exalts celibacy and chastity as ideals rather than as aberrations of human behaviour; a vicious reaction to the sentimentalization of priests in the past, particularly in films and fiction, in great measure as a result of feeling duped and betrayed; and a resurgence of "papaphobia" (a social disorder that sees all political, anthropological and ontological ills originating in the institution of the papacy – *the* arch-deceiver and power monger of history).

Few have managed to capture the contorted and self-contradictory position of these new high priests of condemnation better than Aidan Mathews, an Irish writer, radio commentator, and startlingly original theological savant whose own struggles with mental illness, addiction and professional pressures have generated autobiographical reflections of compelling insight:

> Today the culture teaches my children to beware in turn of Catholic clergymen, and of heterosexual males: just at the moment, estrogen is good, testosterone bad. Just as gay vicars popped up with a regularity that was almost risible in the permanent police line-up of the Sunday newspapers in the 1960s, so today's condemnatory journalism parades the cartoon monsters of dehumanized priests and perverts. Their faces glitter with our saliva – in part the spit of our self-righteous outrage, in part the drool of our prurient obsessions. For there is a deep and unclean psycho-sexual gratification in the work of revulsion. Disgust is the last costume appearance of gusto. And the print and electronic media pander to and profit

from our frothy, foaming incredulity. TV and tabloids are the bully pulpits of a new sacrificial priesthood, as coercive and censorious now as any demonized Maynooth [the great national seminary in Ireland] in the olden times, and these incorruptibles preside as prelates over our orgiastic liturgies of condemnation. For the high-handedness of the prince bishops has been replaced in our day by the hauteur of the puritan divines. (*In the Poorer Quarters*, RTE/Veritas, Dublin, 2007, p. 35)

Mathews is not soft on child-abusing individuals, sacerdotal or otherwise (he has two daughters of his own), nor is he inclined to be defensive of the Church's public image (if anything, his biblical-centred and Celtic-flavoured spirituality has little time for casuistry and canonical double dealing), but he has no stomach for the fickle appetite of the crowd nor for the self-righteousness of the media Sanhedrin. He didn't study under that master genius of the scapegoat and atonement René Girard at Stanford University and learn nothing after all.

Wente's dismissive remark confirms the accuracy of Mathews's observation. But there is a reason and a context for that remark, a reason and a context that have managed to create a wave of national abhorrence. This wave is the direct result of the alleged discovery of child pornography on the laptop of a much-travelled Canadian bishop, Raymond Lahey, Bishop of Antigonish and Chancellor of St. Francis Xavier University in Nova Scotia.

To add insult to injury, this was the same bishop who had managed to achieve an historic out-of-court settlement worth millions of dollars for abuse victims in his diocese. It was an unprecedented move lauded by everyone – lawyers, victims, lay Catholics, political leaders, and fellow bishops – and promised to bring an end to a sad chapter in the region's history. And now, charged with possessing and importing child pornography, the very same bishop whose intelligence, charm, approachability and fairness were admired nationally had now compromised not only his own integrity but that of the episcopal office at a time when it was slowly rehabilitating itself in the public mind, following the protracted debates and legal foot-dragging over culpability and liability in the Residential Schools issue.

The timing was satanic.

Writer Michael Friscolanti puts it in context:

> Though shocking, Lahey's arrest was not exactly surprising. Sadly, he is just the latest in a long, infamous line of Catholic clergymen accused of preying on innocent children (or in his case, watching from afar as others prey on children). The headlines have been repeated so many times over so many years that it's difficult to look at any man in a Roman collar and not assume the worst. *Of course Bishop Lahey had kiddie porn on his computer. All priests are pedophiles* …The media is not to blame for the allegations against Bishop Lahey – or the sins of any other priest who uses his spiritual authority to violate a child … But at the risk of downplaying decades of unspeakable abuse – or forgiving a church hierarchy that move heaven and earth to suppress scandal and protect criminal clergy – an obvious point is often ignored: the vast, vast majority of Catholic priests are not sexual predators. In fact, the scientific research suggests that men who target children are no more pervasive in the priest-

hood (and perhaps less pervasive) than in any other segment of society.

Depending on the study, somewhere between two and four percent of priests have had sexual contact with a minor. Or, to put it another way, between 96 and 98 percent have not. ("The Truth About Priests," *Maclean's*, December 7, 2009)

The data do not support the near mythological perception that the Catholic priesthood is a refuge for sexually maladjusted men who, if not disposed to predation on minors, are at least leering perverts delighting in a vicarious pleasure they condemn harshly from the safety of the pulpit. Yet that myth seems securely locked in the public's consciousness, even among Catholics. Naturally, such negativity has an impact on priestly self-esteem. Few have managed to capture the demoralizing and perplexing dimensions of the new assaults on the priesthood better than Dennis Murphy, a respected church bureaucrat, educator, parish priest, founder of the Institute for Catholic Education in Ontario, retreat giver and counsellor to bishops. He writes,

One of the great paradoxes in the Catholic Church these days is that while survey results tell us that priests are still among the most satisfied and happy in the land, most of the priests I know often feel somewhat battered and beleaguered in the exercise of their ministry. Media coverage of and stigma attached to priests' sexual misconduct, stories of physical, emotional and sexual abuse in Canada's Native residential schools, and tales of financial malfeasance in parish administration cast a shadow over the lives of all the ordained, even though the great majority are innocent of any wrongdoing. Some priests feel that their collective integrity has been undermined by a few of their brothers. Those ordained a number of years have come a long way down from our former lofty position in the Church and society, where we were much admired for virtue and competency that were presumed by most.

Today, even the most virtuous, dedicated and accomplished priest often lives under a cloud of suspicion, if not downright mistrust. (*A View from the Trenches: Ups and Downs of Today's Parish Priest*, Monsignor Dennis Murphy, Novalis, 2009, pp. 13-14)

Although it is true, as Murphy says, that "priests are still among the most satisfied and happy in the land," the fact remains that the optics aren't good and morale is at an all-time low. Priests feel besieged and are besieged. And when a bishop becomes involved in a scandal, a bishop who has a national reputation as a leader and reconciler, the feeling of isolation is compounded. The sense of betrayal is complete.

Pier Giorgio Di Cicco, the Poet Laureate Emeritus of Toronto, essayist, civic aesthetist and prolific writer, is also a priest of the Archdiocese of Toronto. Horrified by the appalling status of the priest in society, the automatic suspicion generated by the very sight of clerical attire, and the irrational attack on the priesthood by the media, Di Cicco was especially incensed by Wente's gross generalization and blanket judgment. He chose to defiantly wear his clerical collar when travelling in public, refusing to be intimidated by stares of disapproval, and to self-identify as a priest rather than seek protection in the literary salon. Margaret Wente's comment was the coup de grâce: no sympathy "for a politician or a priest."

The furor created by Lahey's arrest and subsequent charges resulted in a tsunami of outrage, righteous anger, undisguised venom and despair. The most frequently used word in the media was "devastated," a word used by Catholics and non-Catholics alike, including several Atlantic Canada prelates: the Archbishop of Halifax, Anthony Mancini; the Archbishop of St. John's, Martin Currie; and the Bishop of Charlottetown, Richard Grecco. And it adequately described the national feeling, along with revulsion.

Blogs, websites and letters-to-the-editor pages were replete with opinion and commentary largely hostile to the Church and its clergy. There was little in the way of censoring, and condemnation was swift and merciless. One online comment for the *S.E .Calgary News* is typical of the scores of postings excoriating the Roman clergy and their overseers:

> And what about the multitude of priests, nuns, diocesan employees who knew children were being raped/sodomized/molested and said nothing?

> And what about the priests, nuns, diocesan employees who actually saw children being raped/sodomized/molested and did nothing?

> Until miters and red hats are being put behind bars, nothing, NOTHING will change.

Although the animosity and bile represented by the above were more the norm than the exception in the public sphere, far more potent in its authority and relevance was the kind of editorial solicitation you find in a commentary provided by a professional historian with a reputation for serious scholarship and with earned credibility within the faith community itself. Elizabeth W. McGahan writes in an article for a New Brunswick newspaper that

> the Lahey situation is a metaphor for the worst in a church desperately in need of reform. Clergy personnel in all churches are held to a high standard of conduct; the church's stature has been eroded by the behavior of some of its priests and bishops. And for many faithful Catholics the inescapable impression is that their church has not had enough men in positions of authority with either administrative acumen or pastoral integrity when it mattered most to the laity … United by baptism, committed laity and clergy need to break the silence and begin a forthright conversation on genuine reform at the parish and diocesan levels.
>
> It's reveille for the Catholic Church. (*Telegraph-Journal*, November 6, 2009)

But it isn't only the Canadian Catholic Church that wrestles with the numerous aftershocks of clerical sex abuse scandals. Almost every national jurisdiction is affected, some with greater prominence than others, nearly all living, or trying to live, with the legal, institutional and moral fallout. The United States has dealt with some of the most egregious cases: notorious predators; diocesan bankruptcies; national publicity of a particularly sordid nature. Cumulatively, it has all had a deleterious impact on the church's public image and its capacity to recruit. The U.S. Orthodox priest and writer John Garvey recounts a conversation with a conservative Catholic that is sure to give nightmares to the bishops:

> The Vatican's recent statement that it will create a special ordinariate for Anglicans who want to become Catholics, presumably because of their dissatisfaction with the ordination of women and the elevation of gay bishops, reminds me of a conversation I had with a very conservative Catholic. Following the sex scandals in the Catholic Church, he wanted to become Orthodox. He didn't for a moment want to give up his belief in papal infallibility or any other central Catholic doctrine; he wanted to leave behind an institution that allowed bishops to protect priests who had been guilty of abuse. (*Commonweal*, November 20, 2009)

At the heart of the potential convert to Orthodoxy's dismay with his own Church is his frustration with episcopal authority and its seeming incapacity to exercise the basic rudiments of accountability. And accountability is precisely at the core of the clerical sex abuse scandal that has swept the United States for decades. For months at a time, revelations of priestly misdeeds jostled for frontline coverage with major political events, received the lion's share of investigative assignments, prompted a media blitzkrieg of prolonged and relentless fury, and generated a spate of articles, commentaries and books on sex and Catholicism, sex and celibacy, sex in the confessional, and sex and the Vatican. Sex and Roman Catholicism has always been a titillating subject, drawing in equal measure the attention of the curious, the confounded, the informed and the entrepreneurial. But never has it been as good as this. Or as bad.

The failings – egregious or otherwise – of those consecrated to live a chaste and celibate life have always been fodder for writers, critics and reformers. Read Chaucer. And then read Erasmus. There is a sound Catholic literature of critique and judgment that predates Hans Küng.

But few could have anticipated the cataract of allegations, criminal sentences, judicial blunders and ecclesiastical misjudgments that inundated the United States: very few, but there were some. Catholic journalist Jason Berry wrote many investigative pieces in the mid-1980s for the Kansas City–based *National Catholic Reporter* on the unfolding Louisiana sex scandal involving the priest-pedophile Gilbert Gauthe. In 1985, "The Problem of Sexual Molestation by Roman Catholic Clergy: Meeting the Problem in a Comprehensive and Responsible Manner," a jointly authored report by priest-psychiatrist Michael Peterson, priest-lawyer Thomas Doyle and Monsignor Richard Mouton, was submitted to a meeting of diocesan attorneys and executive committee members of the U.S. Conference of Catholic Bishops, with the understanding that it would be discussed by the full Conference. The executive thought otherwise. That was the first in a series of stunning miscalculations.

By the early 1990s allegations and lawsuits were breaking out across the United States – Dallas, Santa Fe, Fall River (Massachusetts), Los Angeles – and the possibility of an expeditious termination of the unfolding scandal was extremely remote. Guidelines had been drafted as early as 1988 by the U.S. bishops, a policy statement was issued in 1992, and a subcommittee to address clerical sex abuse was formed. But as the scathing and ruthlessly honest National Review Board's "Report: Causes and Context of the Sexual Abuse Crisis" (February 27, 2004) makes clear, "the failure to adopt mandatory guidelines throughout the country and recalcitrance in certain dioceses in implementing voluntary ones despite burgeoning problems set the stage for the current crisis." (*Origins: CNS Documentary Service*, March 11, 2004, p. 662)

And they didn't get much more recalcitrant than the Archdiocese of Boston and its powerful shepherd, Cardinal Bernard F. Law. At the beginning of 2002, information that Law or his delegates had regularly transferred serial pedophiles such as John Geoghan, Joseph Birmingham and Paul Shanley from parish to parish and even outside the archdiocese without apprising the host authorities that they had a predator on their hands created a media storm the like of which Boston had never seen. *The Boston Globe* led the onslaught, but very soon national and international media outlets were camped on-site to record the next sordid revelation, the next pathetic display of clerical mendacity, the next farcical misstep by a cardinal archbishop and his bungling clerical minions as they sought to deploy every legal strategy to prevent full disclosure – the next sad manifestation of pastoral leadership gone rotten. The Boston crisis came to encapsulate all the things that appeared to have gone wrong with a Church run amok, a Church leadership that seemed increasingly to have lost its spiritual moorings, a Church fracturing at its institutional seams.

The Cardinal Archbishop of Boston was, until the death of John Cardinal O'Connor of New York in 2001, the second most influential prelate in the United States.

After O'Connor's death, he was number one, at least for a year. A Yale graduate, a close personal friend of the Bush family (particularly George senior), as well as a friend and confidant of numerous Massachusetts political and business leaders, Law enjoyed close ties with the Vatican, the trust of the pope himself, and the deference, if not the affection, of many of his brother American bishops. This explains, at least in part, the unconscionably long time it took for the Holy See to accept his resignation, in part because Rome's incomprehension of the sex scandal, at least the magnitude of it, was a major reason for the tardiness of response from the head office on the Tiber. Not that Rome is inured to clerical sex scandals – the Vatican authorities have removed, penalized and silenced errant clerics before – but because of the sheer size and pervasiveness of the U.S. problem. The monstrous legal bills, the erosion of the Church's moral authority, the debasing of the image of the priesthood, and the ceaseless media coverage with the concomitant demoralizing of the laity aroused Rome in the end to the extraordinary, if too late, action to restore a modicum of pastoral oversight and order. Law had to go. And, indeed he did go. Eventually, to Rome with an appointment – largely titular – as Archpriest of the Basilica of Santa Maria Maggiore.

The clerical sex abuse malady has erupted in the U.S. Church with particular ferocity, but the Church worldwide – and the Church of Rome prides itself on being a universal or catholic church, the primordial exercise in globalization – has also been infected by the virus. It is tactically insufficient and disingenuous to isolate the problem as a uniquely American or indeed

Western phenomenon. Nor is it appropriate to minimize the damage, bide time before reintroducing the old and established ways of operating, and shelve the issue in the ecclesiastical libraries as a particularly nasty instance of clerical perfidy, like nicholaism (clerical concubinage) and simony (the purchasing of clerical office), abuses of the past that have been largely expunged.

But the debates around the "handling" of the sex abuse crisis continue to expand, polarize and threaten. In effect, the issue has become a proxy for other agendas from various locales in the Catholic ideological spectrum. And, as historian David O'Brien observes, the particularities of the American Catholic culture wars have resulted in an adroit outmaneuvering of the forces of the left by the forces of the right:

> So it was that conservatives won the American Catholic culture wars. They did so by selectively employing counter-cultural language to strengthen Catholic identity and apparently affirm Catholic integrity. They were strengthened by the recruitment of intelligent neo-conservatives and the appointment to leadership positions of Vatican-oriented bishops. But their victory also came about because reformers more or less surrendered. The evidence is all around us: The near total failure of Catholic academic, pastoral and community leaders to take an active role in responding to the sex abuse crisis, the worst scandal in the history of the American church. Of course everyone denounced sin and lamented mismanagement, but reformers chose to leave solutions to the bishops. Many offered formulaic words of encouragement to the lay group, Voice of the Faithful, but very few joined the group or sent in checks; even fewer

formed comparable groups to develop public opinion in the church or contest the ground with the now dominant conservatives. Instead of mature efforts at shared responsibility, they succumbed to the politics of the restored ultramontane hierarchy, exemplified by a cover of the liberal magazine *Commonweal* with a huge ear and the words "Are the Bishops Listening?" In February, 2004, when the remarkably independent National Review Board submitted its reports, no one was ready to use those reports as a basis to demand reforms. Instead there was almost complete disinterest, which continued as the Board was linked more closely to the bishops and their committee.

There are some exceptions to this sad pattern of irresponsibility ... but their limited impact to date simply provides another measure of the completeness of reform defeat. It seems that the same pattern is continuing through the historic waves of buyouts, bankruptcies, court interventions and legislative initiatives aimed at insuring ecclesiastical accountability through the civil arm that has not been provided in the church itself. ("The Missing Piece: The Renewal of Catholic Americanism," Marianist Award Lecture, University of Dayton, 2008, p. 13)

Although O'Brien's point is U.S.-specific, focused on the strategies of reformers and apologists as well as the debilitating consequences of American Catholic ecclesial fractiousness, his analysis is not restricted to the American scene or American history. It finds parallels throughout the world. Catholics are greatly divided by the sex crisis and, depending on their position on the wide spectrum of post–Second Vatican Council Catholic opinion, they either see it as the result of an abject failure to consistently and fully incorporate the teachings of the Council into the life of the Church or they see it as yet another example of the post-conciliar fervour for experimentation, for jettisoning the wisdom of the old, and for the discrediting of authority that continues to threaten the long-term health of the Church. Whatever the label – progressivists versus restorationists, pro-Magisterium Catholics versus liberals, Sedesvacantists versus the orthodox – Catholic thinkers, leaders, teachers, parishioners and commentators all have their views on how the crisis came about, why it festered, and why it was mishandled (for no one disputes that it was mishandled).

In addition, they argue over what role Rome should have played in the unfolding crisis (and on this point all sides agree that Roman intervention should have been swift and immediate), and they argue over what they see as the limitations of professional advice provided by lawyers, therapists, psychologists and psychiatrists over the centrality or non-centrality of the discipline of celibacy (and it is a discipline, not a doctrine), over the evaluative criteria for candidates to the priesthood, over the ongoing sexual education of seminarians, over the existence of homoerotic subcultures in seminaries, and over the place of homosexuals in the priesthood itself.

These arguments are often oracular and generally intolerant of opposing views by coreligionists. Ecclesiastical politics can be much messier than the secular variety. After all, salvation is at stake, not an election.

But if the debates, acrimony and disaffection among U.S. Roman Catholics are receiving the lion's share of global media attention, that does not mean that all is quiet everywhere but the western front. Every front is to some degree roiled.

In Europe, the Hans Hermann Groër Affair dominated the Catholic ecclesiastical scene throughout most of the 1990s. Cardinal Archbishop of Vienna and a former Benedictine Abbot, Groër was accused of having molested young seminarians while in charge of a prominent Austrian Marian shrine years before his appointment as head of the Austrian Church. His rule as archbishop was undistinguished – a mediocre mind and non-charismatic personality, Groër had the ill fortune to follow one of the greatest European churchmen of the century, Franz Koenig – but it was not his personality that was the problem. He did not enjoy the general confidence of his priests, nor, with but one exception, his fellow bishops, either. Then, when he refused to respond to the charges of abuse – neither refuting their legitimacy nor admitting guilt and seeking forgiveness – he alienated hundreds of thousands of Catholics, spawned protest groups that called into question clerical leadership itself, made life increasingly difficult for the Vatican (which managed to deal with the affair in a maladroit and insensitive way that only seriously compounded the problem of authority and accountability), and succeeded with a grand swoop to undo much of what had been accomplished in the post-conciliar years. Quite an achievement.

Resistant for years to every entreaty – internal and external – to tender his resignation or publicly deny the allegations and establish his innocence, Groër was eventually removed by the Vatican once the authorities could see that the irreconcilable divisions created by his continuing presence at the helm stood no chance of being healed. With the bishops increasingly vocal over their unhappiness with Groër, and with radical lay people leaving the church in hitherto unprecedented numbers (they are obligated by law to formally disaffiliate, thereby depriving the church of tax monies), Pope John Paul II appointed a Dominican intellectual and former doctoral student of the then Prefect of the Congregation for the Doctrine of the Faith, Joseph Ratzinger, as Groër's successor. That Dominican friar was Christoph Schönborn. And he had his work cut out for him.

The principal Groër supporter in the hierarchy was Kurt Krenn, himself a controversial bishop who continued to stand by the disgraced Groër, fought the emboldened Catholic laity, encouraged the restoration of Tridentine or traditionalist liturgical practices and devotional mores, lobbied Rome for the appointment of reactionary clerics to leadership positions, and quickly became a thorn in Schönborn's side. In time, Krenn, too, would be required to step down as Bishop of Sankt Polten, less because of his uncollegial style and recalcitrance and more because he was complicit in allowing a decadent sexual culture to flourish in the local seminary.

Although clerical sex abuse scandals arose in other countries besides Austria – in particular, Poland and France – the debacle created by Groër has had long lasting pastoral, moral and political repercussions. Schönborn's handling of the Groër and Krenn aftermath has been in many ways exemplary, but the damage done by the Vatican's tardiness in responding to the scandal has left a bad taste in the mouths of devout Austrians and has seriously diminished public regard for the episcopacy.

In Great Britain, abuse problems arose in several dioceses, including Portsmouth, Brighton-Arundel, Cardiff and Birmingham. Scandal licked at the feet of the very popular and able Cormac Murphy-O'Connor, Primate of the Catholic Church of England and Wales and Cardinal-Archbishop of Westminster. The issue would only really go away following various investigations that established unequivocally that Murphy-O'Connor's handling of a clerical repeat offender displayed incompetence and bad judgment, but not criminal or unethical activity. Like many bishops, Murphy-O'Connor did not appreciate the recidivist nature of pedophilia, the limitations of legal counsel when it comes to protecting the institution's interests, and the inadequacy of psychological treatment to effect a change in behaviour.

In addition to the problems generated by porn-addicted priests, serial abusers and pedophiles, the Church was shaken by several disclosures of sexual impropriety and illegality in two of its most prominent and respected public schools: Ampleforth, administered by the Benedictines, and Stonyhurst, the jewel in the Jesuit educational crown. Although the number of claims were few and the authorities acted with comparative alacrity (compared to the diocesan authorities, that is), one monk perished at his own hands and a beloved Jesuit teacher was jailed. The schools have recovered, recruitment was not imperilled, and trust among the parents and alumni has been in great measure restored. Damage was done, particularly at Stonyhurst, where police investigations dragged on for several years and involved more than one teaching master.

At other schools run by Church orders, clerical or lay, litigation continues. Many abusers have been sentenced. The human damage can be ascertained by the number of addictions, failed lives and suicides among the victims. St. William's Community Home for "troubled" boys near York, in the diocese of Middlesbrough, was run by the De La Salle Brothers, a worldwide order of lay brothers dedicated to teaching. Although the school closed in 1992, over two hundred men have come forward alleging either physical or sexual abuse or both at the hands of the brothers. In 2004, the former Head of St. William's, Brother James Carragher,

> was jailed for 14 years for abusing children, all aged between 10 and 16. He was, said one of the detectives involved in the case, "the most evil of men" who had regularly raped the boys in his care. He had earlier served four years in jail for similar offences. Two of his De La Salle colleagues were acquitted and the cases against another three men were dropped before coming to trial. (*The Observer*, Tracy McVeigh, November 15, 2009)

But what was seen as closure in 2004 has returned to the courts in 2009 with a vengeance.

In what is the largest abuse claim in English Catholic history, 142 men are suing for compensation in the range of some £8 million and a battle royal has broken out between the order and the diocese. The courts have decided that the diocese had the power to appoint staff, and that although the De La Salle Brothers held the senior positions, they were, in the eyes of the law, employed by the Diocese of Middlesbrough. The Brothers deny that they had been the responsible management of St.

William's. And so, amidst the human detritus of several decades of brutalizing behaviour, the fight now being waged is between two discrete ecclesiastical bodies under the one Catholic umbrella. For the media and for the community at large, including most Roman Catholics, these fine points of canonical distinction are seen as a means of evasion, a road to liability avoidance. The moral high ground has simply been abandoned, hijacked by lawyers, vicars-general, curial chancellors temporal, nervous bishops, and insurers of ecclesiastical bodies corporate. Not surprisingly, many Catholics have been dismayed by the juridical approach taken by the Church and see it as yet one more sign of pastoral neglect.

But it isn't quite so simple. It never is.

If the rot at St. William's has proven to be fodder for media consumption by both the qualities and the tabloids – and it assuredly has and continues to be – it pales by comparison with the seismic upheaval experienced by the Church across the Irish Sea.

It all came to a head in the fateful year 2009. Although various documentaries, investigations and reports have been produced on abuse in Catholic-run institutions for a couple of decades following the arrest of the Norbertine Brendan Smith in the 1980s, nothing could have prepared the Irish Church, or, for that matter, the universal Church, for the publication of two detailed reports – the Ryan and the Murphy.

The Ryan Child Abuse Commission Report (named after Justice Sean Ryan), in the eyes of Michael Kelly, Deputy Editor of *The Irish Catholic*, has

> shed light on a reign of terror in Ireland's industrial schools and reformatories where evil had become

endemic. This report stands out as the greatest blot on twentieth-century Ireland and casts a long shadow on Ireland's feeble attempts to construct a truly Republican State based on the values of liberty, equality and fraternity. Looking back now, it is clear that Ireland cast off the shackles of British serfdom and the dreadful British class system to replace it with a petty snobbery that now beggars belief. ("Re-Imagining Catholicism in the Light of Institutional Abuse," John XXIII Distinguished Lecture, November 13, 2009, St. Thomas University, Fredericton, New Brunswick)

The Ryan Report has had an electrifying effect on the Irish population, forcing Catholics, non-Catholics and ex-Catholics to review their history as a nation and as a Church, to re-examine the myths that govern their sense of identity, to explore the deeper and darker recesses of the tribal psyche. Many commentators have been struck by the sexual pathology that seems, at first glance, to be a major determinant of the crisis. This pathology, in extreme forms, translates into pedophilia, but also can be seen undergirding an anthropology that instills dread of sexuality, fosters a truncated spirituality that despises the physical, supports a culture that elevates celibacy over married love, and reduces Catholic morality to bodily purity, with all the rubrics and restraints implied. Michael Kelly observes,

> as I read the names of the more notorious abusers in Canada it became patently and shamefully obvious to me that there was a distinctly Irish dimension to the crisis: Brown, Corrigan, Hickey, Kelley, O'Connor,

Kenney, Maher were among the names of those clerics convicted of abusing children in their care.

In Australia, they included Butler, Claffey, Cleary, Coffey, Connolly, Cox, Farrell, Fitzmaurice, Flynn, Gannon, Jordan, Keating, McGrath, McNamara, Murphy, Nestor, O'Brien, O'Donnell, O'Regan, O'Rourke, Riley, Ryan, Shea, Sullivan, Sweeney, Taylor, and Treacy.

In the United States: Geoghan, Brown, Brett, Conway, Dunn, Hanley, Hughes, Lenehan, McEnany, O'Connor, O'Grady, O'Shea, Riley, Ryan, Shanley.

In Britain: Dooley, Flahive, Jordan, Murphy, O'Brien.

And, of course, all those in Ireland itself.

Irish names are prominent wherever in the English-speaking world clerical child sex abuse has been spoken of. Even allowing for the uniquely high number of Irishmen among Catholic priests and religious worldwide, this phenomenon is striking. Nowhere else in the Catholic world has another nationality been as dominant among clerical child sex abusers. ("Re-Imagining Catholicism in the Light of Institutional Abuse").

Any kind of profiling is dangerous, and any suggestion that Irish people carry within them some kind of "abuse gene" is absurd. But Kelly does raise several points with his lamentable litany of Hibernian miscreants. He rightly notes, drawing on the 2002 Sexual Abuse and Violence in Ireland Report (published by the Dublin Rape Crisis Centre) that abuse is not defined by nor limited to the clergy. The Report found that 30 percent of Irish women and 24 percent of Irish men had been sexually abused as children. This contrasts with 17 percent for women and 5 percent for men in Europe and 29 percent and 7 percent respectively in the U.S. The report also found that a young boy was twice as likely to be sexually abused in Ireland as in any other country.

Even allowing for statistical anomalies, ideological colouration, author bias and incomplete data, the conclusions are damning. The nation's soul-searching exercise must involve a careful analysis of the many constituent parts that make up the problem: the Romanizing of the Celtic spirit; years of conquest and oppression; limited educational opportunities; an imported streak of Puritanism that became a signature dimension of Irish Catholicism – institutionalized and regularized; historical insulation from the great intellectual movements and political events that convulsed Europe; a social and political importance attached to the priesthood that was outside a theological frame of reference.

And then came the Murphy Report.

This report – the result of a government-created Independent Commission of Investigation by Judge Yvonne Murphy – covers the period from January 1975 to May 2004. It deals exclusively with cases that fall within the jurisdiction of the Archdiocese of Dublin alone. The Report declares at the outset:

> The Dublin archdiocese's preoccupations in dealing with cases of child sexual abuse, at least until the mid-1990s, were the maintenance of secrecy, the avoidance of scandal, the protection of the reputation of the church, and the preservation of its assets. All other considerations, including the welfare of

children and justice for victims, were subordinated to these priorities. The archdiocese did not implement its own Canon Law rules and did its best to avoid any application of the law of the state.

In many ways, this is just a local iteration of the universal pattern of response. But there are distinct differences from other like situations, such as the Commission's readiness to identify political complicity: "the state authorities facilitated cover-up by not fulfilling their responsibilities to ensure that the law was applied equally to all and allowing the church institutions to be beyond the reach over the normal law enforcement processes." The Report identifies particular individuals as remiss in the exercise of their duties, principal among them Dublin's Police Commissioner Daniel Costigan ("a number of very senior members of the Gardai regarded priests as being outside their remit") and examined the cases of 46 priests against whom 325 complaints were filed. But the report's release, the politics of composition and reception, the astonishing level of cooperation between the Archbishop of Dublin and the Commission, and the hitherto uncharacteristic level of ecclesiastical transparency are all attributable to the current Archbishop, Diarmuid Martin.

A career Vatican diplomat with many accomplishments under his cincture, Martin was appointed to Dublin to clear up the mess. He wasted no time in doing precisely that. But it hasn't been easy. He promised full and complete disclosure, releasing all the personnel files previously marked confidential, forcing his fellow bishops to engage in direct and public cooperation with the work of the Commission, excluding no one in the process. He was compelled to drag his immediate predecessor, Desmond Cardinal Connell, into the scene. None were to be spared. Connell's level of openness in the past had been extremely cautious. This failure to be fully forthcoming fed the fires of victim hostility, compromised further the withering credibility of the episcopal leadership, and placed the Church in a potentially lethal legal quandary.

It is easy to understand Connell's trepidation. The Murphy Report was unsparing in its criticism of many senior Catholic prelates whom, it argued, conspired for decades to cover up the abuse of children by priests. Among those senior Catholic prelates are Martin's four immediate predecessors: John Charles McQuaid, Dermot Ryan, Kevin McNamara and Desmond Connell himself. But it wasn't just these archbishops – three of whom are now dead – who were identified as remiss in their pastoral duties. Former auxiliary bishops of the archdiocese have been implicated. Several – now serving as bishops of other dioceses – have been obligated to tender their resignations. Principal among them was Donal Murray, Bishop of Limerick, an author, theologian and catechist.

Public outrage can be reasonably gauged by the move of Dublin city councillors to have Archbishop Ryan Park in Dublin's Merrion Square renamed as a "gesture to all of those who have suffered as a result of clerical abuse."

Taken together, the Ryan and Murphy reports – both published in 2009, the *annus horribilis* of the Irish Catholic Church – are the results of comprehensive investigations. The reports are an indictment of ecclesiastical leadership, of a deep moral failure at the heart of the institution's mission, and of strategies of coping that were more cover-up than honest disclosure and healing. Diarmuid Martin's determination to lead Irish Catholics – clergy and laity alike – to a new place, a place where pathologies personal and institutional must be faced, where the rights of victims have priority over the image and reputation of clergy and religious, where justice and love, not cheap mercy and misplaced loyalty, command the highest attention, may lead him in directions that a timid, deferential and preferment-seeking hierarch would fear to tread. Martin has faced sharp criticism from many of his fellow bishops, and has angered many of his priests – not only by his single-mindedness, but also by his peremptory manner, elliptical approach to in-house communications, and glib dismissal of Irish theological acumen. Although Rome accepted two resignations, they confirmed two auxiliary bishops in their positions contra his publicly nuanced wish. Irrespective of his personal management style, Martin remains, if not unblemished, still the premier moral leader to be found in a hierarchy in disarray.

Daniel O'Leary, the much-respected spiritual writer and Irish priest working in the Diocese of Leeds, puts the Irish dilemma in stark terms, and the challenge for reformers in starker tones still:

> A transformation within the Church will not be facilitated by blame and bitterness, but by a realistic acceptance of the role we all play in its dying and its rising. The clerical model of church authority has drifted too far from the vision of the carpenter's son. Commentators refer to the idolatrous pull of power,

privilege and possessions that subtly infect even the most religious organization when an isolating clericalism replaces a loving servanthood.

Strangely, maybe it is in Ireland, in the midst of its painful and devastating meltdown, and maybe indeed because of it, that elements of the truth may be emerging at last. Layfolk and clergy are beginning to speak out their truth in the public forum even if it brings conflict, shock and anguish within their own ranks and across the country. ("Painful but cleansing," *The Tablet*, 16 January 2010)

O'Leary's summons to the Irish Church to become a beacon to the universal Church by learning from its meltdown, perhaps becoming a herald of reform, is at heart both a theological and an ecclesiological challenge. This will be a daunting undertaking requiring a spiritual resourcefulness and intellectual temerity not hitherto much on display in the contemporary Irish Church. However, as *Irish Independent* columnist David Quinn has noted, even though in the short term the Irish Church has learned from the scandals, a Rubicon has been crossed:

Its child protection policy is the most comprehensive of any institution in Ireland. It is more comprehensive even than the state's policy ... Whether the Church will be allowed to move on depends in large part on whether it manages to avoid a diocese-by-diocese nationwide inquiry ... Most people are likely to adopt a wait-and-see approach before they conclude that the Church really is serious about child protection. However, the truth is that even when that day comes, assuming it comes, no Irish person, Catholic or otherwise, will be able to look upon the Church's leaders in the way they once did. ("Sins of the Fathers," *The Tablet*, 5 December 2009)

But old loyalties die hard, if at all. Writer and columnist Mary Kenny, the author of numerous books on the "new" and the "old" Ireland, and an astute critic of the prevailing myths of the Irish, whether self-generated or imposed, made a confession in her column in U.K.-based *The Catholic Herald* shortly after the publication of the Murphy Report. Given the charge that child abuse was widespread in Ireland and the numbers involved both monstrous and incredible, she wondered why an Irish society so "notoriously gossipy [and] making private jokes about so many matters never leaked a word?" The Ireland that Kenny knows and loves is not the Ireland of recent making, although the seeds of that making were clearly fecund.

Simultaneously, the church was wrestling with the ongoing investigation into the Legionaries of Christ (LCs), described by many in a language similar to that used by Britain's *The Independent*, as "a shadowy but powerful Catholic sect, which was founded by the charismatic Mexican priest Marcial Maciel Degollado." The LCs undoubtedly have structural and ascetical similarities with a sect – unquestioned obedience to and reverence for the Founder; a heavy cloak of secrecy around its internal and external operations; interventions into the private lives of its members; severe sanctions for actual or perceived disloyalty; lack of transparency concerning financial matters. But in fact it is a canonically established religious community with full approbation by the Congregation for the Institutes of Consecrated Life and Societies of Apostolic Life and with the approval of the Vatican.

The Legionaries have numerous property holdings, large reserves of cash, lucrative international investments, many seminaries and universities, an expanding pool of students for the priesthood, a powerful lay affiliate body, Regnum Christi, and an extraordinary network of social and political connections in many countries, especially Mexico.

Most importantly, the LCs were much admired for their devotion to the Holy See, "orthodox" spirituality, personal generosity to the Holy Father and his causes, and exponential growth when most religious orders and congregations have been experiencing serious decline for decades. The LCs held a Vatican "favoured son" status and they delighted in it.

However, for many years, dating back to the 1950s, a cloud of suspicion hung over the head of Maciel, although variously dissipated and scattered. He was regularly the object of allegations of sex abuse by seminarians, ex-seminarians, priests and former Legionaries, but no progress was ever made. The allegations were neither proved nor disproved, the rumours ever proliferating then dying down, only to be resurrected anew.

Maciel enjoyed – and revelled in – a privileged relationship with John Paul II.

He did not enjoy a similar relationship with Benedict XVI, formerly Joseph Ratzinger.

In fact, shortly after his accession to the papacy, Benedict suspended Maciel from the public exercise of his priestly ministry, consigned him to a penitential place, and watched fearfully as the fabric of skillfully woven lies unravelled with unsettling speed following Maciel's death in 2008.

The rumours proved to be true; the accusations were confirmed; the length and breadth of Maciel's perfidy were exposed to all – in his order and in the world. The founder of the Legionaries of Christ – known among his disciples simply as the Father – led a double life. He fathered several children (at least one of whom is suing the Legionaries), had many lovers, sexually abused countless seminarians and priests, and amassed a private fortune.

Benedict put the Legion under the control of a special delegate of the Vatican and established a commission to reconstitute or reformulate the way the order operates:

> the very serious and objectively immoral behaviour of Father Maciel, as incontrovertible evidence has confirmed, sometimes resulted in actual crimes, and manifests a life devoid of scruples and of genuine religious sentiment. The great majority of Legionaries were unaware of this life, above all because of the system of relationships built by Father Maciel, who had skillfully managed to build up alibis, to gain the trust, the confidence and silence of those around him, and to strengthen his role as a charismatic founder.

That the words used by the Vatican itself to describe the acts of the founder of the Legionaries could also be used with only slight modification to describe abuse throughout the world was not lost on most observers.

In addition to allegations about the LCs in Mexico and Spain, there were rumours and charges in Brazil,

Bolivia, Uruguay and Chile involving sexual abuse, rape and other brutalities.

But there was much more going on than simply within the ambit of the beleaguered Legionaries.

At the end of January 2010, allegations of abuse – emotional, physical and sexual – by priests in Germany, Austria and Belgium began to be unearthed. Jesuit college schools began to surface complaints of abuse, followed in short order by a cataract of allegations from almost every one of Germany's 27 dioceses.

By March of 2010, victims began to number in the hundreds, if not in the thousands; the tally of perpetrators moved from the dozens to the hundreds. There were also allegations regarding the physical abuse of choir boys launched against the pope's brother, Msgr. Georg Ratzinger, choirmaster at the Regensburger Domspatzen. Even Germany's Chancellor, Angela Merkel, entered the fray: "the sexual abuse of children ... is an abhorrent crime ... there is only one possibility for our society to come to grips with these cases: truth and clarity about all that has happened."

Indeed, the operative word has become "all." With the clamouring for full disclosure has come a concomitant sense of outrage and anger at every perceived effort at obstruction or evasion.

Back in Canada, the public's anger over the revelations following Bishop Lahey's resignation was sustained for several days, fuelled by a media frenzy usually accorded genocidal maniacs, disgraced press barons, stubborn and evasive former prime ministers, and befuddled host-consuming politicians. But this anger was deeper, visceral, tinged by self-righteousness and disproportionate. This observation is not intended to diminish the gravity of the issue or to make a special case for an otherwise exemplary religious. It is only to marvel at the intensity and ferocity of the coverage itself.

The Globe and Mail, Canada's premier newspaper of record, thundered in its leader of October 9, 2009:

> It is heartbreaking that Roman Catholic parishioners in this country are being made, once again, to feel abandoned by their leadership ... The fact that his parishioners were taken by surprise in this way – some described it as being "punched in the stomach" – is eloquent testimony to the long-standing evasiveness that Canada's Catholic Church has engaged in with regard to the sexual victimization of children.
>
> This tendency, over and over and over, to down play, stonewall, and foot-drag rather than assume clear and unequivocal leadership simply has to come to an end.
>
> We are not speaking, after all, of allegations of money laundering or bicycle theft. The extremely brave Canadian police investigators who are made to look at images of child pornography will tell you that these are not Playboy-style images of naked children. They are images that depict devastating acts of violation and cruelty perpetrated against our most vulnerable, the young ... what is required now is extraordinary eloquence. Parishioners need to know that the Church shares the public's revulsion at such behaviours and will minister to the abiding pain so many of their sons and daughters have experienced in the past decades, rather than deepen it.

Who would argue against what must appear as measured anger? Who would gainsay the high moral tone taken by the paper? And who could possibly remain unpersuaded by the sweet reasonableness of its logic?

But a careful examination of the rhetorical tropes, the undeclared biases, the oracular tone, the condescending and judgmental attitude demonstrated towards church authorities, and the false assumptions concerning church initiatives and accomplishments that are operative throughout the editorial argument, all provide evidence that the emotional high road taken by *The Globe and Mail* merits a detailed and sustained analysis.

To understand what has transpired and why, to set the recent spate of scandals within a larger framework of consideration, to explore the underlying causes that have perpetuated injustice and to suggest ways forward are at the core of an agenda for reform.

Who writes that narrative is, of course, the key question of this work.

4

What We Actually Mean When We Talk About Abuse

In an irony that has not gone unnoticed, the arrest and laying of charges against Bishop Lahey in the fall of 2009 caused simply one more tremor in a major convulsion in the worldwide Catholic Church during a year the Vatican designated "Year of the Priest."

What became clear was that the Year of the Priest abuse scandals varied by country, circumstance and detail, but are remarkably similar at the heart of both what was going on and how it was and would be perceived within the Church and outside it.

Lewis Carroll, aka Charles Lutwidge Dodgson, was a master of mathematical and linguistic puzzles. His masterpiece, *Alice in Wonderland*, contains at least two exchanges that touch directly on how vitally important it is to get things right when we toss around terms and ideas.

In an encounter between Alice and the March Hare at the Mad Hatters' Tea Party, we are forced to wrestle with this clear admonition:

"Then you should say what you mean," the March Hare went on.

"I do, " Alice hastily replied; "at least I mean what I say, that's the same thing, you know.

"Not the same thing a bit!" said the Hatter. "Why, you might just as well say that "I see what I eat" is the same thing as "I eat what I see!"

And as if that rather astute observation on the difficulty of expressing ideas wasn't challenging enough, Alice's confrontation with Humpty Dumpty raises the matter to a new level altogether.

"When I use a word," Humpty Dumpty said, in a rather scornful tone, "it means just what I choose it to mean – neither more nor less."

"The question is," said Alice, "whether you can make words mean so many different things."

"The question is," said Humpty Dumpty, "which is to be master – that's all."

Making sense of the clerical abuse scandal requires that we be clear on what is and what isn't going on when clerics are charged with and convicted of committing acts of abuse. All abuse is wrong, but different types of abuse have different origins, pathologies and treatments. There are distinctions between types. Being clear on distinctions helps us focus on what can and what should be done to address the causes. In this chapter and in the chapter on the history of the sexual abuse scandal, we will explore some of these distinctions.

In *The Globe and Mail* of March 11, 2010, there appeared on page 12 a short news account of a press conference held by a coalition of eighteen Ontario police forces. According to the story, the press conference was called to announce the latest results of a province-wide initiative aimed at child pornography. Thirty-five people in Ontario had been charged with 122 counts of child porn. Ontario Police Commissioner Julian Fantino declared at the event that "This is a crime that, to me, is one of the most heinous one human being can commit against another." He went on to say that "police will stop at nothing to hunt down child predators."

Despite the relatively slight prominence given to the announcement by "Canada's national newspaper," especially given the view of a senior police officer that the crimes involved were heinous, and given *The Globe and Mail*'s treatment of the charging of Bishop Lahey, the details of the investigation and the charges were quite alarming.

The 35 accused ranged in age from the late teens to the early 60s, came from "all walks of life," had no previous criminal records and were not part of a ring. One of the accused had six million images of child pornography stored on his computer, an amount that one of the officers involved in the case, Staff-Sergeant Frank Goldschmidt, described as "not uncommon" for child pornography collectors.

The charges laid against Bishop Lahey in the fall of 2009 are arguably the least of the sins alleged against the Church and its members. This is not to diminish what he is alleged to have done. Yet , over time, our understanding of pornography and its consequences has changed and continues to change. Understanding and getting to the root of abuse by clerics requires being clear about what it is we are talking about. In a world of three-word headlines and the use of hype and exaggeration to attract readers and viewers, it is especially urgent that we create room for distinction and degree. If words become interchangeable, if definitions blur, if we accept a laziness of mind, speech and conclusion, we risk dealing unjustly with everyone involved.

The heart of the matter is the question, the idea, the accusation and the reality of abuse. "The scandal" that is rocking the Roman Catholic Church around the world is layered, nuanced and multi-faceted. It goes deep into our understanding of morality, legality, responsibility, accountability, sins of omission and commission, and above all what we mean when we use words, even words as seemingly straightforward as "abuse."

Legal niceties aside, pornography is of course a sin in Christian eyes, and the exploitation of children a matter much condemned. If the language of sin is seldom found or heard in the media, where a 'legitimate' linkage can be made with sin (and what more legitimate linkage than a case involving a cleric), the temperature of the reporting heats up. That might explain why the charging of Raymond Lahey made worldwide news while the charging of Bill Surkis, former head of the Quebec Branch of B'nai Brith, and the conviction of Master Corporal Donald Costin of Essex remained local stories. The reality is that even the most heinous of offences is not without context.

The March 5, 2010, edition of the *The Art Newspaper* carried a brief news story on its front page with this intriguing headline: "Curators Cleared in Child Porn Case." In 2000, the Bordeaux Museum of Contemporary Art was home to the exhibit "Presumed Innocent: Contemporary Art and Childhood." A children's charity in France, La Mouette, complained to the police that the exhibit contained "pornographic images of children." After a lengthy investigation, a French magistrate ordered that the director of the École Nationale Supérieure des Beaux-Arts, Henry Claude Cousseau, a Louvre curator, Marie-Laure Bernadac, and Stephanie Moisdon, who curated the show in question, be tried on charges of child pornography. According to news accounts, the court of appeal threw out the case in part because "some of the disputed works have been already shown in other prestigious museums worldwide such as MoMA in New York." It is not the first time, nor will it be the last, that well-meaning individuals disagree on what is and what isn't child pornography.

In 2009, Christopher Handley, a 39-year-old Iowa office manager, pled guilty to "possession of obscene visual representations of the sexual abuse of children." The charges stemmed from Mr. Handley's importation of seven Japanese comic books. As numerous news accounts, including *Wired* magazine's story "U.S. Manga Obscenity Conviction Roils Comics World," noted, Handley was the first person ever convicted under the U.S. 2003 "Protect Act," which makes it an offence to possess or distribute "cartoons, drawings, sculptures or paintings depicting minors engaging in sexually explicit conduct."

Also, in 2009, a huge battle broke out over the attempts by Wyoming County Pennsylvania District

Attorney George Skumanick Jr. to use child pornography laws against three teenage girls who were using cell phones to send nude photos of themselves. According to reports at Law.com, the district attorney "threatened to prosecute the three girls on child pornography charges for their roles in the creation of two digital photographs unless their parents agree to place the girls on probation and send them to a five-week, 10-hour 're-education' program in which the girls must discuss why their conduct was wrong and 'what it means to be a girl.'"

Child pornography is a crime of abuse with a particular twist. There is a distance between the abuser and the abused. While child protection groups, police forces, prosecutors and legislators rightly point out that there are real victims of child pornography and that consumers of child pornography create a market that necessitates a continuing supply of new victims, most viewers of child pornography have no intimate or physical contact with the abuse victim.

Child pornography, as separate from other forms of abuse, has an additional distinction. The consumption of pornography generally is a massive enterprise worldwide. Tens of millions of people consume pornography daily around the world. It's available in most hotel rooms in North America under the label of "adult content." It is one of the largest profit centres of pay-TV channels and is by far the most prominent of uses of the Internet. It is an industry that measures global revenues in the trillions of dollars. One estimate puts pornographic consumption at $3,000 per second worldwide.

In fact, pornography has become almost commonplace. In 2007, Telus, one of Canada's largest cellular phone providers, announced plans to make possible the distribution of pornography over cell phones. From the company's perspective, the distribution of porn over the phone seemed like a normal business plan designed to service a market. It took outrage, denunciation and the Archbishop of Vancouver's threat to organize an institutional and personal boycott of the phone company to force the company to reconsider and ultimately scrap its plans.

As discussed in Chapter Three, "A World in Flames," we live in a sex-saturated society. Sex is used to sell everything and anything, and sexualizing a situation or context seems sadly inevitable. This seems especially true as we confront the increasing use of sexualized images of children.

In the spectrum of the sexualization of human beings, pornography is often seen, depending on one's moral, psychological or political stance, as liberating, as the commodification of yet one more sphere of reality, as demeaning of the object and consumer of pornography, or as a sin.

Child pornography remains the one area in the world of porn that is punished relatively severely, is seen as abhorrent by most, even among consumers of pornography, and is viewed as evidence of deviant behaviour, psychological disorder and/or an addictive personality. The reasons explaining the consumption of child pornography are murky. Criminal justice perspectives are evolving; the consequences for consumers, producers and victims a matter of some contention.

Every conversation about child pornography raises real problems of definition, as we can clearly see in the context of the charges against Bishop Lahey. But talking about the reality of clerical sexual abuse is a minefield. And this becomes starkly clear when we sort out the different meanings and beliefs about the phenomenon of clerical abuse as it has occurred throughout the world.

Trying to determine what clerical sexual abuse means to the Church, the perpetrators, the victims and society at large necessitates tackling the easy issues first.

There is a depressingly similar pattern to the allegations of abuse, regardless of geography. The abuse occurs in institutions, involving vulnerable children brought together because of status: orphans, disabled children, troubled individuals, Aboriginal children. The abuse takes place in contexts perceived by all to be safe, supervised by trusted members of the Church: choirs, organized league activities, charitable works, pastoral duties and religious education exercises. The abuse takes a number of forms: physical, emotional and sexual. Rumours of the abuse circulate for some time as gossip and innuendo. Complaints to police are dismissed as hysterical ramblings by disturbed individuals. Civil and Church authorities at first deny the possibility. The matter is often left to the Church or its institutions to follow up. Abusers are often treated in a manner that facilitates or even enables subsequent abuse. The victims suffer intense physical, emotional and psychological pain. A culture of silence, secrecy, denial or obfuscation ensues. Eventually, the sheer weight of allegation, charge, rumour, insistence and obvious pain and suffering result in the story emerging. A media barrage erupts. Church officials, civil authorities, criminal courts and civil lawsuits wrestle with the fallout. Entire dioceses are forced into bankruptcy in a less than adequate attempt to provide reparation for what turns out to have been decades of abuse. And we all hope that that is the end of the story.

This has been the case in Louisiana, Massachusetts, Newfoundland, England and Australia. It was the case with Canada's residential schools, and it appears to be the path that Ireland will travel. Germany, Austria and Belgium are themselves clearly set on a course that will be far too familiar to Catholics in London, Boston, Brisbane and Antigonish.

What is not truly clear is how this situation differs for the Catholic Church from stories of abuse in other contexts: sports coaches, the American Boy Scouts, too many schools *not* run by the Catholic Church to count, Buddhist sanghas, military academies or foreign aid workers. When the sex abuse scandal first emerged in Germany, *Der Speigel*, a leading German publication, noted that abuse allegations were arising from institutions other than Catholic ones, which led to the question "How widespread is sexual abuse in Germany?" It is a question that pertains to all circumstances.

Despite the fact that our perception of the clerical sexual abuse scandal fixes its emergence in the mid-1980s with the case of Father Gilbert Gauthe in Louisiana, numerous historians have tried to make clear that the reality is much, much older. Of course, regardless of when we want to date the eruption of the scandal, the accounts of abuse stretch back over much of the 20th century. Ireland is struggling with a 60-year history of abuse, with no indications that it didn't stretch back further. Canada's shame of residential schools originates in the 19th century.

Father Thomas Doyle, a Dominican priest, canon lawyer and former member of the staff of the Papal Nuncio to America, is without doubt a controversial figure. Much loved by abuse victims' organizations, hated by many conservative Catholics, and in an awkward relationship with his order and the U.S. bishops, Doyle was one of the first to warn in 1985 of the shape and range of the unfolding scandal. In March of 2010, he posted online at the website of the Crusade Against Clergy Abuse a remarkably detailed examination of the Church's history of wrestling with clerical sexual misbehaviour. Entitled "A Very Short History of Clergy Sexual Abuse in the Catholic Church," the article is in fact a dense, fact-filled eight pages outlining the reasons for and the nature of the Church's difficult and mixed record of confronting the problem, beginning with the Council of Elvira in 306 AD.

If there is a common thread running through a 1,700-year history that helps us today, it is simply this. The crisis that began 35 years ago is the first to seek solutions from civil authorities and civil and criminal courts. What once might have been seen as an internal Church matter between institution and laity, authority and victim, is now in public view and subject to other authorities.

One consequence of the new and very public nature of the sexual abuse scandals is the perception that it is widespread. Going from unreported and secret to open and everywhere has led to a sense that the whole Church is mired in open and soon to be open scandal.

Terms such as "epidemic," when used in news accounts, lead everyone to conclude that abuse is the norm and a non-abusive cleric the exception. In reality, of course, the situation is the exact opposite.

In May of 2010, Sally Jenkins, a columnist for the *Washington Post*, wrote, "It's a difficult, even upsetting question, because it risks demonizing scores of decent, guiltless men. But we've got to ask it, because something is going on here – there's a disturbing association, and surely we're just as obliged to address it ...."

She went on to quote Jay Coakley, a sociologist from the University of Colorado: "We can no longer dismiss these actions as representative of a few bad apples. The evidence suggests that they are connected to particular group cultures that are in need of critical assessment."

But Jenkins wasn't writing about the newest twist in the clerical abuse scandal. She was writing about the latest news story involving male university athletes and the horrifying statistics on assaults, physical and sexual, being committed by men who might simply be responding to the culture they are immersed in. And Jay Coakley doesn't write about the Church but is the author of *Sport in Society: Issues and Controversies*.

It should be no relief to Catholics or the Church that other systems and institutions are as likely to breed abuse, but it should suggest to us all that reflection and refraining from a rush to judgment are worthy activities at the best and worst of times.

Studies done in the 1990s in the U.S. and Canada have found that the percentage of priests who have abused children ranges from 1.8% to 4%. When compared to the population at large, the numbers are actually at the low end of the scale. The statistics on sexual and other forms of abuse in society as a whole clearly indicate that there are far more dangerous places for vulnerable young people to be than in a church or Church-run institution. And whereas churches are often described as places of trust and perceived safety, and therefore the fact that abuse occurs is more heinous, the sad reality is that abuse most often takes place in the home, and the abuser is most likely a relative.

Naturally, the statistics, while reassuring, do not mean that clerical sexual abuse is not a problem. Nor do these statistics offer an argument that because the Church is no worse than the rest of society, this is a reason to be complacent or defensive. But the numbers do play a role in separating out myths and misperceptions about the nature of the problem and hint at the real nature of the crisis facing the Church both internally and with the wider public.

Historically, the evidence is that anyone of any age might be a victim of clerical sexual abuse. Yet the majority of the victims in the most recent cases have been young boys. This situation has tended to provoke extreme confusion about the nature of the abuse and the reasons for the abuse. That the confusion is not just among the laity or the population at large, but also among Church officials, is clear from a series of missteps by official and unofficial spokesmen for the Vatican. Is this about pedophilia? Is this rooted in homosexuality? Are these crimes of opportunity or a pattern indicating some more fundamental corruption?

Despite the popular media's charge that the Church is going through a pedophilia crisis, the evidence is that most of the reported cases of abuse do not involve pedophilia, nor are many of the abusers pedophiliacs. Philip Jenkins, author of the groundbreaking work *Pedophiles and Priests: Anatomy of a Contemporary Crisis* (Oxford University Press, 2001), has spent more than a decade trying to correct public and media misperceptions about the nature and extent of the abuse scandal. Jenkins's critics, including Catholic scholar Gary Wills, argue that making these types of distinctions is a diversion from the nature of the real problem. Gregory Herek, a professor of psychology at the University of California at Davis, takes a middle-ground approach:

> Although the terms are not always applied consistently, it is useful to distinguish between pedophiles/hebephiles and child molesters/abusers. Pedophilia and hebephilia are diagnostic labels that refer to psychological attractions. Not all pedophiles and hebephiles actually molest children; an adult can be attracted to children or adolescents without ever actually engaging in sexual contact with them.

> Child molestation and child sexual abuse refer to actions, and don't imply a particular psychological makeup or motive on the part of the perpetrator. Not all incidents of child sexual abuse are perpetrated by pedophiles or hebephiles; in some cases, the perpetrator has other motives for his or her actions and does not manifest an ongoing pattern of sexual attraction to children.

> Thus, not all child sexual abuse is perpetrated by pedophiles (or hebephiles) and not all pedophiles and hebephiles actually commit abuse. Consequently, it is important to use terminology carefully.

Another problem related to terminology arises because sexual abuse of male children by adult men is often referred to as "homosexual molestation." The adjective "homosexual" (or "heterosexual," when a man abuses a female child) refers to the victim's gender in relation to that of the perpetrator. Unfortunately, people sometimes mistakenly interpret it as referring to the perpetrator's sexual orientation.

To avoid this confusion, it is preferable to refer to men's sexual abuse of boys with the more accurate label of male-male molestation. Similarly, it is preferable to refer to men's abuse of girls as male-female molestation. These labels are more accurate because they describe the sex of the individuals involved but don't implicitly convey unwarranted assumptions about the perpetrator's sexual orientation.

While disputes about pedophilia vs. ephebophilia or hebephiles may interest the linguists among us or provide ammunition for both Church defenders and critics, the reality is that every case of abuse by clerics, however it is characterized, has only been the beginning of the trauma. As horrible as the individual acts have been, it is the subsequent behaviour of the institution and its officials that has legitimately provoked the true horror among Catholics and non-Catholics alike.

Again, while the details of the abuse committed in Irish institutions, German schools, the Mount Cashel orphanage, the parishes of Louisiana or Massachusetts, the dioceses of Antigonish or Pembroke, the private quarters of the Legionaries of Christ or the school for the deaf in Milwaukee are unique in themselves, there is an aspect to the cases that is consistent and universal. At some point, the crime morphed into a large institutional crime. Just as Watergate began as a botched burglary and transformed into presidential corruption, in the abuse scandal the preying on the young has transformed into a tale of broader and, if possible, more troubling dimensions.

In all the stories that have emerged in the last three decades, at some point it became clear that bishops have known or suspected that an abuser or abusers were operating within the bishops' jurisdictions. Bishops are the focal point for dealing with abuse. They are responsible for the health of the diocese, in all senses of the word, and that includes personnel issues. They assign, evaluate and supervise priests. Concerns about performance, suitability and behaviour are all within the bishop's purview. It is reasonable and was obviously the case that victims of abuse would seek justice through the bishop's office.

The Church is a layered institution with a flow chart that might make all but the most assiduous organizational expert dizzy and confused. The Church is both a decentralized and deeply hierarchical society. It is governed by rules and procedures that have evolved over 2,000 years and has its own norms, codes and legal systems. It has a culture steeped in tradition, ritual and secrecy, as well as a language and modes of discourse that are clear to insiders and opaque to the rest of the world. And, like all institutions, the Church is concerned with its own well-being as much as it is concerned with its mission on earth. As with all institutions, much depends on leadership.

Father Thomas Reese is a Jesuit theologian at the Woodstock Theological Center at Georgetown University.

In a column in the *Washington Post* on May 3, 2010, that deals with the crackdown on the Legionaries of Christ, he contrasted the leadership of Benedict XVI and John Paul II:

> Having grown up in a persecuted church where unity was a matter of survival, John Paul could not accept open debate and discussion in the church. Loyalty was more important than intelligence or pastoral skill. As a result, the quality of bishops appointed under him declined, as did the competence of people working in the Vatican. But the sad truth is that while he was good for the world, he was bad for the church. His suppression of theological discussion and debate, his insensitivity to women's issues, and his appointments kept the church from responding pastorally and intelligently not only to the sexual abuse crisis but to other issues facing the church.

Not everyone accepts Reese's emphasis on the alleged lapses of John Paul II's pontificate. In fact, as we will see, the apportionment of responsibility between, say, John Paul II and Benedict XVI, or between Rome and local bishops, is an argument about the nature of the scandal facing the Church. It is a struggle that takes place inside and outside the Church, but most intensely inside the Church and most publicly outside. It is a struggle that leaves no one untouched.

The novelist and essayist James Carroll, a former priest, has written extensively about Church history and the impact of the sexual abuse scandal on American Catholicism. While generally sharing the opinion that at the crux of the problem is an institution intent on cover-up, he goes one step further and lays some of the blame with the ordinary Catholic parishioner. In his book *Practicing Catholic*, a heart-wrenching account of the difficulties and joys of being an Irish-American Catholic, Carroll argues that Catholics hear the news about sexual abuse and the disturbing pattern of bishops seemingly protecting the abusers differently than others do:

> For us, the devastation and anger involved a measure of personal remorse. It was not only that our entire Church stood indicted – from its system of authority to its clerical culture to its tradition of secrecy to its basic teachings about morality – but also that each Catholic had reason to feel implicated. I am not talking about a generalized corporate guilt here, nor do I mean to take away from the particular responsibility of the individual perpetrators. But the massive failure could not have happened if we the Church had not enabled it.

Living in Boston, Carroll was at ground zero of some of the most egregious incidents of clerical abuse in America. The actions of one bishop in particular, Cardinal Bernard Law, serves as an example of a form of behaviour that seems to mark all the known incidents of sexual abuse. As mentioned in an earlier chapter, in the '80s, the '90s and into the 21st century, Cardinal Law dealt with numerous cases of alleged sexual abuse. He did so by imposing silence on victims, transferring priests who were abusers, intimidating the media and civil authorities when rumours began to fly, and ultimately shielding some of the most egregious predators imaginable. By all accounts, he did so in order to protect the Church from scandal and financial liability and because it was how bishops dealt with the abuse problem. At one point, the Attorney General of Massachusetts concluded that Cardinal Law would have been indicted as an accomplice in the abuse crimes if it weren't for certain technicalities that prevented such an action. The Attorney General was clear that he believed the Boston Church was involved in a cover-up of crimes. Cardinal Law resigned and moved to Rome. Ultimately, Carroll and others saw even this development as evidence of an even greater cover-up. "But, as he had protected abusive priests, the Vatican protected him. Law was named archpriest of the Basilica of St. Mary Major in Rome by Pope John Paul II. It is no wonder. In pursuing his illegal policy of obfuscation, denial, and protection, Law was carrying out instructions from the Vatican itself."

The story of Cardinal Bernard Law and the Archdiocese of Boston is repeated around the world: the ugly, horrible stories of abuse, the apparent efforts to minimize and keep quiet the scandal, and the double horror when the facts become public. The sin and crime of sexually violating a vulnerable person is made that much worse by the evidence of institutional indifference or suggestions of complicity, a disturbing mixture of commission and omission.

Sorting out the various wrongs at work in the clerical sex abuse scandal is important. Getting what went wrong right creates the opportunity to fix what needs to be fixed. As we will see, getting what went wrong right has not been the hallmark of this whole scandal.

5

Constructing the Narrative

One of the great students and practitioners of journalism, E.B. White, once observed that the objectivity so highly and often touted by the media as one of its key attributes and most compelling strengths might rest on a falsehood: "I have yet to see a piece of writing, political or non-political, that does not have a slant. All writing slants the way a writer leans, and no man is born perpendicular."

It is an instructive perspective and one that needs to be kept in mind while following and integrating the news, analysis and conclusions offered about the clerical abuse scandal. We are social beings. We both individually and collectively make sense of the world by amassing detail, facts and impressions. We can get lost in separating out the wheat from the chaff, so to speak. As discussed earlier, perspective and story construction may be everything when it comes to making sense of anything.

The clerical sexual abuse scandal is many things, but it is also a story. The emergence of the details, context, characters, actions, reactions and consequences are fashioned into stories. Making sense of the scandal is as much about making sense of the stories told, as it is anything. Truth exists, but truth is told. In the telling, it acquires its own rhythms, nuances, meanings, shades of meaning and impact.

Whenever we wrestle with drama and crime, sin and punishment, heroes and villains, we are separating meaning from misdirection, understanding from the fog of confusion, a path forward from a blind alley. E.B. White, the great storyteller, journalist and expert in style and language, is on to a masterful idea. No one tells a story straight; some come closer than others, but all must acknowledge that a perspective is at work, a philosophy is at play, a task is at hand. Making sense of what's what is as much a part of attending to a story as it is the heart of telling a story.

In November of 2009, two months after the arrest of Bishop Raymond Lahey, Linden MacIntyre, a celebrated Canadian journalist, won the Scotiabank Giller Prize for excellence in Canadian literature. His novel, *The Bishop's Man*, as mentioned in Chapter Two, is the story of a middle-aged priest confronted by, surrounded by and nearly drowning in accusations about clerical sex abuse as well as its reality. Set in the very diocese where Raymond Lahey had reached the ground-breaking settlement of compensation for 50 years of clerical crimes, *The Bishop's Man* is a bleak tale with redemption a far-fetched idea.

It is smartly written and exceptionally timely. It tapped into and exploited the zeitgeist. The Giller Prize jurors noted, when awarding the $50,000 that accompany the award,

> *The Bishop's Man* centres on a sensitive topic – the sexual abuses perpetrated by Catholic priests on the innocent children in their care. Father Duncan, the first person narrator, has been his bishop's dutiful enforcer, employed to check the excesses of priests and, crucially, to suppress the evidence. But as events veer out of control, he is forced into painful self-knowledge as family, community and friendship are torn apart under the strain of suspicion, obsession and guilt. A brave novel, conceived and written with impressive delicacy and understanding.

In an age where the expression 'ripped from the headlines' is a compliment, MacIntyre, who made his name as Canada's leading investigative journalist, had struck literary oil. He had produced a work of imagination that readers and critics ultimately read as being more true than true. In interviews leading up to being awarded the imprimatur of best novel of the year, and in interviews afterwards, MacIntyre was as likely to be asked his opinion on the exploding sexual abuse scandal as on the agonies of writing prose. In fact, as the crisis leapt from Ireland to Germany, from a school for the deaf to the chambers of the Vatican, Linden MacIntyre became the go-to guy for giving yet another story on the scandal a new twist.

At the end of April 2010, word spread quickly on Hollywood gossip sites that a deal had been reached by a production company and the Boston Globe to produce a feature film telling the story of the *Boston Globe* Spotlight Team's investigation into clerical sexual abuse in Boston in 2002. One website, Deadline, used this headline to break the story: "'ALL THE POPE'S PRIESTS'? Deal to Develop Catholic Church Scandal Film from POV of Boston Globe Journalism Team."

Mike Fleming, the reporter on the story went on to observe,

> The producers intend to frame the movie in the vein of *All the President's Men*. One of the planned film's hooks is that some of the journalists are themselves Catholic and were conflicted as they researched and wrote their stories. This journalism angle seems a fascinating way to approach the topic. And, interestingly, the *Boston Globe* investigative team was headed by Ben Bradlee, Jr., son of the legendary *Washington Post* editor who stood behind Bob Woodward and Carl Bernstein when their Watergate reporting was assailed by Richard Nixon's White House.

Given that the producers have chosen to "frame the movie in the vein of *All the President's Men*," it is not difficult to imagine the basic elements of the proposed movie: brave, honest journalists expose corrupt institution, bringing justice to victims, judgment to the perpetrators and glory to themselves. After all, that's what *All the President's Men*, which documented the story of the *Washington Post* and its exposure of corruption in the Nixon administration, was all about.

Fair is fair. The *Boston Globe* deserves all the credit it gets for its reportage in 2002. Even George Weigel, the conservative papal biographer and Church historian, credits the *Boston Globe* and the media in general with doing the Church an incredible "favour" in exposing true and real corruption and sin in the earlier part of the decade. The modern clerical abuse scandal is traced back to the 1980s, when the first glimpses of how shocking, widespread and complicated the scandal would prove to be emerged. Unfortunately for everyone involved, the basic elements would stay the same through the decades until today.

Innocent children, usually boys, but not always, would be hunted, groomed and preyed upon by men with serious psycho-sexual problems, serial predators targeting the vulnerable. Eventually, rumours, allegations and even evidence would be brought to a Church official. The predator's superior would attempt to silence the victims and their families, wrestle with the priest's behaviour, and counsel penance, therapy or a combination of the two. Then, in consultation with the hierarchy, or often on their own initiative, the predator's superior would decide to reassign the predator to a position away from the original victim. As incidents mounted, it was as if a sense of panic set in. Serial transfers of the serial predator became the norm, along with intensifying efforts to keep a lid on a boiling, roiling horror for victims and the Church. The particular details differ in each horror, but the basic factual framework is sadly universal.

Facts in the beginning of the 21st century have lost much of their hardness and concreteness, becoming more malleable, more contextual than definitional. We live in an age of information overload and spin. The combination of these two truth-adverse conditions are proving deadly to thinking clearly about and navigating through the full dimensions of the clerical abuse scandal. Is the refusal of Cardinal Ratzinger to laicize a priest who is abusing children a cover-up, an act of protection, a self-interested decision, an attention to Church rules and law, or a strategy to protect future victims by ensuring that the predator remains under the Church's supervision? Facts seldom arrive without baggage. Long after they have been supplanted, the baggage remains.

Information overload became a fact of life with the emergence of 24-hour cable news channels and the World Wide Web. Marshall McLuhan, a Canadian Catholic with a keen understanding of communications theory, described for us in the 1960s the world that would be born as the century ended: a global village, with all the good and bad that that concept entailed. What once might have taken months or weeks to be known across an ocean or around the world is now broadcast, discussed and dissected within hours, minutes and seconds. There is little intellectual room available for discernment, reflection or contemplation. Rendering judgment as the facts are still emerging has become the norm of our age.

A case in point: In June of 2009, the Vatican published Benedict XVI's encyclical *Charity in Truth* (*Caritas in Veritate*). Within minutes, the substance and import of the 157-page social treatise was the focus of talk shows on CNN, BBC, CBC and thousands of online blogs and chat rooms. Despite the obvious truth that most, if not all, of the commentators had not had sufficient time to read, let alone reflect upon, the heart of the matter, the battle lines were clearly being drawn. For some, it was a welcome introduction of morality and ethics into the world of high finance and a troubled economy. For others, it was an unwarranted expansion of a suspect tendency on the part of the Church to engage in social justice.

And as the cycle of comment, reaction and comment escalated, an ideological battle ensued. Any one commentator's view on another's stance was seen as evidence of ideological posturing and ultimately a crude litmus test of positions on global warming, immigration, abortion, and capitalism vs. socialism. As is the norm for this age of instant communication, the intellectual disagreements quickly degenerated into vitriol, blanket condemnations and the staking out of extreme positions seldom justified by facts or logic.

The encyclical, years in the making, was reduced to simply a metaphor for a host of other issues and a shibboleth for purposes of staking out turf on the ideological battleground. Compared to what has unfolded in the media coverage of the sexual abuse scandal, the shifting arguments and vitriol over *Charity in Truth* seem the model of decorum and the ultimate in reason.

The tsunami of information that floods over us every minute of every day is in some senses inimical to the idea of truth. Information is neither the definition of truth nor its equivalent. The axiom 'the truth shall set you free' refers to something beyond mere information, though clearly information is a necessary ingredient. Unfortunately, information seldom arrives pure and without that other great inhibitor of our age: spin.

Arguably, spin has been with us since we first began telling stories. Some philosophers claim that stories without spin are impossible. And they have a point. No narrative can exist without a perspective. Stories are told through the eyes of someone. Spin, the idea of casting facts and incidents into a perspective that serves some agenda, is a more modern phenomenon.

The American historian Daniel Boorstin, in his 1961 work, *The Image*, first identified what has become the essence of modern communication. In *The Image*, Boorstin tackles the packaging of politicians, the creation of 'psuedo-events', the marketing of celebrities, and other tools of the public relations industry as they were migrating from the world of advertising to the world of social communications. The reality is that 50 years on, spin is ubiquitous and practised by everyone.

Spin has evolved to the point that now everyone seems gripped by its necessity. As we will see, everyone who grapples with the sex abuse scandal does so from a particular perspective, and marshals fact, perhaps even manipulates facts, to suit a particular argument. A critical characteristic of spin is that no one believes that they practise it, while at the same time believing everyone else practises nothing but spin. Trying to make sense of the scandal while navigating towards wisdom is difficult. A guide to navigation can be discovered in examining aspects of the scandal and the different camps of spin that emerged as the scandal dominated the news cycle from the fall of 2009 to early summer 2010.

Making sense of story selection in journalism might be seen as similar to making law and sausage. As Otto Von Bismarck is reputed to have said, "To retain respect for sausages and laws, one must not watch them in the making." No one denies the importance of journalism and a free press to the proper functioning of a democracy. But, as with any institution, the gap between the ideal and the theoretical and the day-to-day functioning can be a gaping chasm. You can lose sight of the link between the screaming headlines in the sleazy tabloid and the sentiment that led Thomas Jefferson to observe that "were it left to me to decide whether we should have a government without newspapers or newspapers without a government, I should not hesitate a moment to prefer the latter."

Most people outside the profession, and especially people and institutions that find themselves the object of journalistic attention, inevitably confront or raise questions or suspicions of bias, ignorance, attitude and fairness. Journalists and journalism organizations seldom feel the need to explain how or why they go about the work they do.

At the heart of all non-journalistic confusion – and, to be fair, a significant amount of confusion within the world of journalism – is a fundamental question: What makes news *news*? It is not a simple proposition. Far too often, news editors rely on the sense contained within a statement by Justice Potter Stewart, of the U.S. Supreme Court, who observed in a decision on pornography that it may be hard to define, but that he was confident that "I know it when I see it."

Journalists are human beings who come to their jobs with all the biases, ignorance, strengths, weaknesses and noble and ignoble motivations that everyone else brings to their jobs and lives. They are no better, and no worse, than the rest of the population as individuals or as a group. But there is one significant difference between most journalists and the general population. Journalists tend to be more skeptical and more oppositional than the average person. They tend to dispute the accepted wisdom of the day and tend to be distrustful of authority.

Journalism is largely about telling stories. What human beings know about storytelling suggests that stories work best when conflict is present. Stories also function best with characters; good guys, bad guys, victims, villains, heroes and, ultimately, a resolution along the lines of hero saves the day and gets the girl.

In order to fully understand the journalistic treatment of the clerical abuse story, we need to consider the nature of the changes that have seized journalism over the past three decades. The invention of 24-hour news cycles, which took place when CNN hit the airwaves in 1980, changed forever how news emerges and achieves staying power.

TV news is by definition more sensational and dramatic than print news. TV news is more simplistic than long-form analysis. TV news in a 24-hour environment is faster, more superficial and more flighty. But as with any type of inflationary pressure, TV's 24-hour news changes the nature of all news. News is a business. News outlets compete with one another for audience, influence and advertising revenue.

If the arrival of 24-hour news wasn't disruptive enough to the world of news, the emergence of Internet-based news sites, sources, blogs and aggregators changed the nature of news even more dramatically. Now the speed of news is measured in minutes and page clicks. Added to the mix of sensationalism that cable TV news networks brought is an intensification of opinion as news, which emerged with sites such as The Drudge Report and Huffington Post.

The clerical abuse scandal has been reported over time through a variety of journalistic prisms: traditional media treatment in the late '70s through to the mid '80s, the hyper television news wars of the 1990s through to the mid 2000s, and this latest round, in the era of Internet-influenced news coverage. As we have seen, the result has been that, over time, the coverage has become more intense, hysterical, extreme and rooted as much in vitriol as in fact and analysis.

News is a competitive business. News outlets and journalists want to be both of the pack and ahead of the pack, but never behind the pack. At story meetings in the newsroom, what other outlets are or are not attending to is often as much a part of the story selection process as the intrinsic nature of the story itself. Everyone is intent on advancing the story. Everyone needs a new element, preferably an especially dramatic new element, and everyone wants to be the first to bring the new element to the fore. Stories live and die on the basis of injecting a new angle that makes everyone else follow.

The rush these days in news is to be first, sensational, dramatic and, if possible, controversial and provocative. The default position is to side with a victim and distrust an authority. Speed is preferable over thoroughness, exposé over explanation, and stark over nuanced. Complicated, layered, intricate and perplexing stories without clear, definitive conclusions are not necessarily ignored, but they rise to the top of the news agenda only if the difficult elements can be replaced by the preferred qualities.

Finally, it should be noted that the media strive to be the definitive maker of narrative. Truth telling is a competitive enterprise in the age we inhabit. As we will see, the clearest example of this confrontation over who gets to define what about the evolution of the clerical abuse scandal is taking place between the *New York Times* and the Vatican.

"Nothing happens in isolation" should be the first axiom of any attempt to understand what we know, why we know it and how. The sexual abuse scandal isn't happening in isolation. The arrest and charging of Bishop Raymond Lahey was both a bolt from the blue and not. The dramatic 'shocking news' aspect to the story is an invention of the media. Each charge of sexual malfeasance directed at a cleric is treated as if it was a completely new subject. Every new allegation is 'evidence' of a widespread problem, regardless of when the alleged incident occurred. Despite detailed references to exposés going back three decades or longer, the sexual abuse scandal is reported as fresh and current. This is meta-spin at its most fascinating.

The media have their own language, mores and habits of behaviour. Breaking news isn't simply a branding slogan; it is a mantra that accentuates immediacy. Immediacy demands constant attention, and the media feed on constant attention. So when news of the impending charges against Bishop Lahey broke, the strictly accurate reporting of the matter was "Canada-wide Warrant Issued for Bishop" and "Bishop's Location Unknown." Both were true statements and both were hyped to the nth degree. Canada-wide warrants are issued daily in this country for a range of crimes. Bishop Lahey's location was unknown, though we soon realized it was simply because he was on his way to surrender to police. Similarly, much was made about where the bishop might live while on bail. There was a remarkable flurry of attention paid to a rumour that he might be at a monastery in New Brunswick. What was never made clear was why the bishop's location was important. In a universe of 'breaking developments,' every move, every breath, every rumour becomes the stuff of bulletins and one more reason why you need to keep your television on whatever channel brought you the latest tidbit.

In the winter of 2010, the media's approach to news and the consequent filtering that flows from the values of modern-day journalism clashed head on with the Church's approach, or at least the Church hierarchy's approach, to both the scandal itself and how best to communicate around it. It can be described fairly as an ugly scene. Many observers believed it was best captured in what became known as The Vatican vs. *The New York Times*.

In the early days of Lent 2010, news stories out of Germany suggested that a scandal similar to those in the United States and Ireland was beginning to emerge in Pope Benedict's native land. Amid accounts of rampant abuse at a Jesuit-run high school and reports of priest predators on the prowl in German schools, choirs and orphanages, one account alleged that Cardinal Joseph Ratzinger might have been involved in dealing out suspect special treatment to a priest predator in the diocese of Munich and Freising. In media parlance, this is known as a smoking gun. The rush to link the present pope to the mess of scandals worldwide was on.

It probably should go without saying that the way in which the pope is treated by the secular media is different from the way he is perceived or treated by Catholic media or Catholics themselves. For a billion Catholics, the pope is the pontiff, the head of the Church – the moral, spiritual and organizational leader of the faithful and the institution created to lead them. For non-Catholics, the pope is at best a popular beloved leader of one of the world's great religions, and at worst a man steeped in arcane mysteries who wears odd clothing and leads an organization rumoured to be wealthy beyond imagination, governed by peculiar rules and rooted in myths and beliefs long abandoned by more sane human beings. At the best of times, the pope is celebrated as a man of peace and a force for great good. At the worst of times, well, the sex abuse scandal was clearly the worst of times. In the early months of 2010, it quickly became clear to the Vatican, to Catholics at large and to the world how the pope was characterized in the worst of times.

With stories of the pope's role as a bishop in Germany or, for the last 20 years of the century, as Prefect of the Congregation for the Doctrine of the Faith (and nominally responsible for rooting out clerical wrongdoing), the media smelled blood and the pope became a target. In effect, Benedict as Ratzinger became the key piece in a puzzle that, once completed, would show the Catholic Church to be an institution that harboured priest predators and sacrificed all to protect the institution. And would do so even if that meant obstructing justice, trampling on the victims and evading moral, criminal, legal and financial responsibility for crimes too numerous to count and to heinous to be believed. From the Vatican's perspective, it was a narrative tale in the style of *All the President's Men*, and Benedict was cast in the role of Richard Nixon.

On the other hand, the media did believe that the continuing revelations of systemic abuse in country after country, in tales of remarkable consistency, with just the names of the innocent and guilty being changed, demonstrated a pattern, a structural problem, an institution that must be actively engaged in organized corruption, or how else might this all be understood?

And so it was that *The New York Times* began to devote considerable resources to documenting the unfolding story of clerical abuse in Europe, the reaction in the Vatican and developments in the United States. In a provocative series of reports dealing with the horrible case of Father Lawrence Murphy, a priest at St. John's School for the Deaf in Milwaukee between 1950 and 1974 who was alleged to have molested nearly 200 young boys, the *Times* suggested that Cardinal Ratzinger, at the time Prefect of the Congregation for The Faith, intervened to prevent Father Murphy from being tried before a canonical court. *The Times* was implying that the future pope was engaged in a cover-up.

The story proved to be too much for Cardinal William J. Levada, the former bishop of San Francisco who succeeded Cardinal Ratzinger as Prefect of the Congregation. In a long letter released to the public, sent to *The New York Times* and published in *The Catholic San Francisco*, Cardinal Levada began by saying as an American, he was not proud of "America's newspaper of record, *The New York Times*, as a paragon of fairness." He went on to identify exactly how he thought the reporter, Laurie Goodstein, and the editorial board of the paper had failed its readers.

The New York Times presents both a lengthy article by Laurie Goodstein, a senior columnist, headlined "Warned About Abuse, Vatican Failed to Defrock Priest," and an accompanying editorial entitled "The Pope and the Pedophilia Scandal," in which the editors call the Goodstein article **a disturbing report** [emphasis in original] as a basis for their own charges against the Pope. Both the article and the editorial are deficient by any reasonable standards of fairness that Americans have every right and expectation to find in their major media reporting.

The cardinal went on to detail what he saw as leaps of logic, cascading charges and the conflating of details and assertions in an attempt to indict the pope. In particular, Cardinal Levada challenged the mixing up of timelines, when the abuse was reported, lines of communication, to whom the abuse was reported, as well as mixing allegations in lawsuits and unchallenged facts in a way as to equate the two. In his statement, he noted,

In her lead paragraph, Goodstein relies on what she describes as "newly unearthed files" to point out what the Vatican (i.e. then Cardinal Ratzinger and his Congregation for the Doctrine of the Faith) did not do – "defrock Fr. Murphy." Breaking news, apparently. Only after eight paragraphs of purple prose does Goodstein reveal that Fr. Murphy, who criminally abused as many as 200 deaf children while working at a school in the Milwaukee Archdiocese from 1950 to 1974, "not only was never tried or disciplined by the church's own justice system, but also got a pass from the police and prosecutors who ignored reports from his victims, according to the documents and interviews with victims."

Reflecting for a moment on his own personal knowledge of Benedict, he concluded:

> But about a man with and for whom I have the privilege of working, as his "successor" Prefect, a pope whose encyclicals on love and hope and economic virtue have both surprised us and made us think, whose weekly catecheses and Holy Week homilies inspire us, and yes, whose pro-active work to help the Church deal effectively with the sexual abuse of minors continues to enable us today, I ask the *Times* to reconsider its attack mode about Pope Benedict XVI and give the world a more balanced view of a leader it can and should count on.

Cardinal Levada's challenge to *The New York Times* shifted the focus of much of the media's coverage. He touched an emerging theme that suggested that media reporting and commenting on the abuse crisis had taken on the hue of anti-Catholicism. Flippant observations about papal dress, the 'club of old men,' and the tarring of all clerics with the brush of actual or potential desire for young boys made many Catholics and non-Catholics nervous. And in the world of secular and religious press, more and more writers and pundits were wondering if there was something else at play beyond the clear and tragic story of abused children and an organization that might be engaged in an alleged cover-up.

Now it seemed as if, instead of reporting on a sad and challenging period in the Church's history, the real story was a square-off between a largely secular press and the Church as an institution. It probably didn't surprise the cardinal that the public editor of *The New York Times* rejected the claims of unfairness.

Kenneth L. Woodward, a former editor of *Newsweek* magazine and a prominent Catholic writer, captured the mood of a shift in the nature of the coverage in a essay published in *Commonweal* magazine entitled "Church of the 'Times': A Dissent." After reviewing the way the *Times* and other media had dealt with the sex abuse scandal, he concluded,

> No, I am not suggesting that the scandal is merely media-driven, as some at the Vatican have argued. There would be no stories if there had been no history of abuses and cover-ups in the first place. But I am saying that the *Times* has created its own version of the scandal as if they had discovered something new. They haven't. Until they do, I remain a dissenter in the pews of the Church of the *New York Times*.

In the Church vs. the Secular Media, the end result is a standoff. Neither trusts the other to speak the truth or to behave honestly. As a consequence, the media believe they are dealing with a corrupt institution that is resistant to reform and that is engaged in obfuscation and illegality. The Church and its most passionate defenders believe the media are not honest brokers but entities bent on the destruction of the Church, indifferent to the precepts and tenets of religion, and fixated on forcing the Church into the media's own vision of law and order – ultimately hoping to lay all responsibility at the feet of Benedict.

The media timetable and the media universe of rules and assumptions are but two aspects of the spin and narrative of the sex abuse scandal. There are many others. It is important to keep in mind that while the sexual abuse scandal is real, not everything about the sexual abuse scandal is really about the sexual abuse scandal.

The first decade of the 21st century was marked by an intensification of the old argument about the role of religion in society. The attacks of September 11th reminded the planet that deadly zeal inspired by theological injunction could bring entire peoples to the brink of all-out war. In addition to forcing all people of faith to examine their consciences, the image of the collapsing Twin Towers of New York gave added impetus to the power of the emerging New Atheism movement. The obvious power of Islamist ideology and the willingness to use violence of all kinds to implement the same had alarmed a part of the world that had come to believe that religion was an evolutionary backwater on the road to eventual extinction. Sam Harris, Richard Dawkins and Christopher Hitchens were the cheerleaders of a self-styled group of humanists bound and determined to finally eradicate religion as an institutional force, a personal comfort or even an acceptable point of conversation among enlightened educated people.

The New Atheists wove together three strands of anger. Scientists, shocked at the creationists/intelligent design opponents of Darwinian thought, quickly hooked up with ideological opponents of Christian Right politicians and preachers and found common cause with Western intellectuals manning the barricades for the final showdown with Islamic jihadists. The lowest common denominator for these three disparate perspectives was the demonization and ultimate eradication of religion. The clerical sexual abuse scandal was the secular equivalent of manna from heaven. With venomous prose, they circled in for the feast.

Sam Harris, author of *The End of Faith*, in an essay in May of 2010 posted on The Huffington Post, wrote,

> I confess that, as a critic of religion, I have paid too little attention to the sexual abuse scandal in the Catholic Church. Frankly, it always felt unsportsmanlike to shoot so large and languorous a fish in so tiny a barrel. This scandal was one of the most spectacular "own goals" in the history of religion, and there seemed to be no need to deride faith at its most vulnerable and self-abased. Even in retrospect, it is easy to understand the impulse to avert one's eyes: Just imagine a pious mother and father sending their beloved child to the Church of a Thousand Hands for spiritual instruction, only to have him raped and terrified into silence by threats of hell. And then imagine this occurring to tens of thousands of children in our own time – and to children beyond reckoning for over a thousand years. The spectacle of faith so utterly misplaced, and so fully betrayed, is simply too depressing to think about.

Richard Dawkins, an evolutionary biologist and author who is sometimes known as "Darwin's Rottweiler," has moved 180 degrees on the clerical abuse scandal. In *The God Delusion*, published in 2006, Dawkins wrote,

> Priestly abuse of children is nowadays taken to mean sexual abuse, and I feel obliged, at the outset, to get the whole matter of sexual abuse into proportion and out of the way. Others have noted that we live in a time of hysteria about pedophilia, a mob psychology that calls to mind the Salem witch-hunts of 1692. The Roman Catholic Church has borne a heavy share of such retrospective opprobrium. For all sorts

of reasons I dislike the Roman Catholic Church. But I dislike unfairness even more, and I can't help wondering whether this one institution has been unfairly demonized over the issue, especially in Ireland and America.

But in April of 2010, Dawkins weighed in on the scandal, writing that Benedict was a "leering old villain in a frock, who spent decades conspiring behind closed doors for the position he now holds ... a man whose first instinct when his priests are caught with their pants down is to cover up the scandal and damn the young victims to silence."

Christopher Hitchens, a self-described contrarian and author of numerous books and essays attacking religion generally, but Catholicism and Islam in particular, went for the jugular when he wrote,

> The Roman Catholic Church is headed by a mediocre Bavarian bureaucrat once tasked with the concealment of the foulest iniquity, whose ineptitude in that job now shows him to us as a man personally and professionally responsible for enabling a filthy wave of crime. Ratzinger himself may be banal, but his whole career has the stench of evil – a clinging and systematic evil that is beyond the power of exorcism to dispel. What is needed is not medieval incantation but the application of justice – and speedily at that.

Over-the-top rhetoric, perhaps, but this trinity of dedicated enemies of not just the Church but of all religion made clear their real agenda when they announced plans to attempt to have Benedict XVI arrested when he went on a papal tour of England. In a bold publicity stunt, the three announced a strategy to seize Benedict and bring him before the International Criminal Court in The Hague on charges of crimes against humanity. All of this proved to be too much for the folks at *Spiked*, a British humanist publication normally not ideologically sympathetic to the Church or religion. In April of 2010, *Spiked*'s editor Brendan O'Neill, in an editorial entitled "Why Humanists Shouldn't Join in This Catholic Bashing," said, "The discussion of a relatively rare phenomenon as a 'great evil' of our age shows that child abuse in Catholic churches has been turned into a morality tale – about the dangers of belief and of hierarchical institutions and the need for more state and other forms of intervention into religious institutions and even religious families."

But the narrative spin of the New Atheists is by no means the only story being told.

In March of 2010, the controversial and famous theologian Hans Küng, in a series of letters and essays as well as several interviews, weighed in on the storm of allegations, charges and counter-charges rocking America, Ireland and Europe. Acknowledging that abuse was widespread in society and welcoming the efforts on the part of the Vatican and national churches to apologize and clear the air on the historical instances of abuse, he went on to identify what he saw as the structural and doctrinal explanations for why the abuse was happening within the Church:

> Compulsory celibacy is the principal reason for today's catastrophic shortage of priests, for the fatal neglect of eucharistic celebration, and for the tragic breakdown of personal pastoral ministry in many places. Abolition of the celibacy rule, the root of all

these evils, and the admission of women to ordination. The bishops know this, but they do not have the courage to say it in public.

Küng, a contemporary of Pope Benedict XVI, was disciplined by the Vatican in 1979. His right to teach theology in Catholic insitutions was removed as a result of his opinions and teachings denying papal infallibility. Küng is a leading intellectual among reformers who are intent on systemic change in the Church. In April, he continued his reflections on the abuse scandal in an open letter to the Catholic bishops. He wrote, "there is no denying the fact that the world wide system of covering up sexual crimes committed by clerics was engineered by the Roman Congregation for the Doctrine of the Faith under Cardinal Ratzinger between 1981 and 2005."

Küng's all-too-familiar public stances proved too much for George Weigel, the conservative American theologian and papal biographer. In an open letter of his own, published in *First Things*, Weigel accused Küng of a career-long exercise in personal aggrandizement and then turned to Küng's attacks on Benedict:

> That, sir, is not true. I refuse to believe that you knew this to be false and wrote it anyway, for that would mean you had willfully condemned yourself as a liar. But on the assumption that you did not know this sentence to be a tissue of falsehoods, then you are so manifestly ignorant of how competencies over abuse cases were assigned in the Roman Curia *prior to Ratzinger's seizing control of the process and bringing it under CDF's competence in 2001*, then you have forfeited any claim to be taken seriously on this, or indeed any

other matter involving the Roman Curia and the central governance of the Catholic Church.

In this singular set of exchanges, two of the most important narrative spins surrounding the current clerical abuse scandal are revealed. George Weigel and Hans Küng can be seen as representative of a long, engaged argument within the Church about the past and the future. For both individuals and the perspectives they embody, the clerical abuse scandal is terribly real and the result of serious theological and structural flaws. The abuse scandal is one more battleground. As a result, the arguments, assessments and conclusions about the scandal put forward in essays, columns, interviews and quotations are not innocent of spin or narrative agendas. The issues are real, the arguments sincere. Identifying a narrative spin doesn't rob them of validity. Discovering the biases is simply part of the process of navigating through a complex traumatic story.

The 'liberal reform' perspective, often represented in publications such as *The Tablet*, *Commonweal* and *The National Catholic Reporter*, sees the roots of the abuse in compulsory celibacy and the Church's refusal to ordain women. The cover-ups that seem to inevitably follow the abuse are linked to institutional prerogatives, a centralizing authority in Rome and a quarter-century worth of bishop appointments where loyalty mattered more than thought. The scandal is hurtful and a threat to the Church and the faithful, but it can be dealt with.

The conservative reform perspective, often represented in publications such as *The Catholic Herald* in the United Kingdom and *First Things* and *The National Catholic Register* in the United States, sees the roots of the abuse in a failure to root out homosexuality in the priesthood, a slackening in moral standards within modern society and among the Catholic laity, and weakness on the part of Rome and bishops around the world to enforce the clear teachings and commandments of the faith. Broad generalizations about factions and perspectives are at best an entry point into what is known in the parlance of the 1970s as media literacy. While we swim in a sea of media, we need to use at least a portion of our time coming to grips with the quality of the quantity of media we absorb. The irony of the information overload we experience on a daily basis is that more information may lead to less exposure to differing views and perspectives. The explosion of new sources of information has led to a greater fragmentation of information sources. A growing body of evidence suggests that more and more individuals read and absorb information that tends to confirm what they already believe. So the New Atheists tend to read each other rather than reading religious writers who might shed different or new perspectives on the role of religion in the 21st century. Liberal reformists tend to read journals and bloggers that confirm their perspectives, while dismissing the opinions and perspectives of conservative reformers – and, of course, vice versa. Secular media outlets discount religious media as tainted and biased, while religious media outlets worry that secular media are blind to their own inherent biases.

Who do you trust? What do you believe? The sexual abuse scandal is deeply troubling, regardless of where you start. But one thing is certain. Navigating through the flood of fact, opinion, perspective, spin and narrative guises is an important part of coming to grips with the crisis. Beware of simple answers and definitive explanations, as both are probably rooted in deeper, more complex questions. We do know one thing for certain. Leaving everything up to others has only resulted in us being where we are today. As Albert Einstein once observed, "Insanity: doing the same thing over and over again and expecting different results."

6

The Crisis and the Response

The Roman Catholic Church could be forgiven for thinking that it's not quite fair that it gets singled out for all the attention over sex when so many other institutions appear to be spared a comparably intense global scrutiny.

Certainly, the military (Colonel Russell Williams in Canada), other churches (the Pentecostals and Assemblies of God in the United States, with Jimmy Swaggart, Jim and Tammy Faye Bakker, and other lesser televangelists in the 1980s and 1990s), and political leaders (Maxime Bernier in Canada, U.S. federal and state senators, state representatives and congressmen such as Roy Asburn, Larry Craig, Bob Allen, Richard Curtis, Mark Foley, John Edwards, Eliot Spitzer, to name but a few) have had their day in the sun, but none has had the relentless exposure to a blistering media focus that has been accorded Catholicism.

Still, there are key differences involved: the electorate has become inured to the fallibilities of politicians, the hypocrisies of religious frauds, and the machinations of military sociopaths. But the Catholic Church's centuries-old mystique, exotic power structure, sacralized priesthood, impressive organizational apparatus, icons of holiness and charismatic personalities all make the "sins of the Fathers" especially heinous.

Certainly, the betrayal of trust is all the more destructive when one is dealing with a model such as a priest compared to a hockey coach, Big Brother, family friend, Boy Scout leader, and so on. It cuts to the heart of one's spirituality, confounds one's understanding of God as merciful and all loving, tears apart one's capacity to taste of God's forgiveness when God's own instruments – the priests – are the prime perpetrators of one's ravaged innocence, leaving a trail of psychological scars that may never heal. In other words, the damage is all the greater when the authority figure represents God.

An editorial in *The Globe and Mail* of March 25, 2010, put it bluntly:

> The Catholic Church is not the only large organization with pedophiles amongst its members; however, it is one of the few that systematically protected sexual predators. The Pope must send a decisive signal that this era is over and reforms are in place to ensure clerics who abuse children and adolescents are removed. The Abbot of the Benedictine Abbey in Einsiedeln, Switzerland, has suggested creating a central Vatican registry for pedophile priests to prevent them from being shuffled from one parish to another. This would represent a meaningful next step. Prayer, fasting and apologies are not enough. Transparency and accountability are needed.

When a whole community, a whole nation, feels collectively betrayed, spiritually violated, the damage is enormous. The need to do more than fast, pray and apologize is obscenely evident – as in Ireland. By looking closely at the current Hibernian trauma in this chapter and in Chapter Eight – and it is indubitably a trauma – we can draw important lessons for all other jurisdictions similarly disabled by a leadership in disarray, by a poverty of imagination at the highest levels, and by the urgent need to channel lay and clerical – yes, clerical – anger.

Still reeling from the unending tremors generated by the Murphy and Ryan reports, the entire Irish episcopate's emergency meeting with the pontiff in Rome, and internal turmoil among some of the bishops who chose to close ranks rather than tender resignations, the Irish nation found itself at the receiving end of an unprecedented papal apology, but an apology with more than a mite of unwelcome nuance and qualification.

In his pastoral letter of March 19, 2010, the feast day of St. Joseph and the name day of Joseph Ratzinger, a humbled pope made clear his purpose for writing: "considering the gravity of these offences, [the abuse of children and vulnerable young people by members of the Church in Ireland] and the often inadequate response to them on the part of the ecclesiastical authorities in your country, I have decided to write this pastoral letter to express my closeness to you and to propose a path of healing, renewal and reparation."

The pope identified among the key contributing factors to the current crisis the following:

> inadequate procedures for determining the suitability of candidates for the priesthood and the religious life;

insufficient human, moral, intellectual and spiritual formation in seminaries and novitiates; a tendency in society to favour the clergy and other authority figures; and a misplaced concern for the reputation of the Church and the avoidance of scandal, resulting in failure to apply existing canonical penalties and to safeguard the dignity of every person.

In addition, Benedict addresses individually the victims of abuse and their families, the parents, children and young people of Ireland, the priests and religious of the country, his brother bishops, and all the faithful of Ireland. He proposes initiatives of both a specifically spiritual and a juridical focus – time to pray for God's mercy; enhanced opportunity for Eucharistic adoration; a nationwide mission for all the bishops, priests and religious of the nation; the particular invocation of St. John Mary Vianney, the Curé d'Ars; and an apostolic visitation of certain dioceses, seminaries and religious congregations throughout Ireland.

He is especially direct when speaking to the bishops: "grave errors of judgement were made and failures of leadership occurred. All this has seriously undermined your credibility and effectiveness ... Only decisive action carried out with complete honesty and transparency will restore the respect and goodwill of the Irish people towards the Church to which we have consecrated our lives."

Few have doubted the pope's sincerity, sorrow and solicitude. The letter was a strikingly forthright and quick response to a deeply disturbing pathology. But the response from many Catholics in Ireland and abroad was twofold: the pope did not exact any immediate costs for failed stewardship, and he did not demand the resignations of those bishops whose egregious inattention or mishandling of the problem in their own diocese merited strong official reprimand. Rather, he identified various factors that spoke to a diminishment of religious ardour, a laxity among Irish Catholics in the practice of the faith because of a misguided post–Second Vatican Council openness: "all too often, the sacramental and devotional practices that sustain faith and enable it to grow, such as frequent confession, daily prayer and annual retreats, were neglected … The program of renewal proposed by the Second Vatican Council was sometimes misinterpreted and indeed, in the light of the profound social changes that were taking place, it was far from easy to know how best to implement it." His words prompted many loyal Catholics to see this diagnosis as an effort to exculpate in part the clergy by blaming the culture and the Council.

The prominent British Catholic Martin Prendergast spoke for many when he thundered in a letter to the editor of *The Tablet* (March 27, 2010),

> one sees, in the letter, the hand of those elements committed to backtracking on the reforms of Vatican II … This is a scandalous insinuation that the conciliar reforms somehow colluded in creating such levels of abuse. Had the Council's vision of episcopal collegiality and co-responsibility for the mission of the church with all the people of God been pursued with honesty and transparency, such structural dysfunction might have been prevented.

But Prendergast's anger pales by comparison with *The Irish Independent's* John Cooney, in a piece that appeared on March 22, 2010:

> not only did the pope not commend the Irish State for conducting the Ferns, Ryan and Murphy Commissions which outed clerical abusers and the bishops' cover-ups, he trotted out the main excuse for the bishops' long inaction that was discredited by Judge Yvonne Murphy – that they did not understand the scale or criminality of child abuse until recently … Not only did Benedict not apologize for the refusals of the Congregation for the Doctrine of the Faith and the papal nuncio to respond to queries from the Murphy Commission, he has extended his remit into the sovereign jurisdiction of the Irish State by pledging to hold an apostolic visitation, a secretive, Vatican-led inspection of unspecified dioceses, religious orders and seminaries in Ireland.

Cooney, a respected but severe critic of Irish Catholicism, is excessive in his condemnation of Benedict. The pope is entirely within his right to conduct an ecclesiastical inquiry that deals directly with canonical and spiritual matters. In fact, several Irish bishops tendered their resignations in the immediate aftermath of the Murphy report's release. But the vexatious tension between the Church and state authorities over access to confidential files being sought by the Commissioners – particularly the Murphy Commission – and the adamant opposition to cooperation with the civil authorities characteristic of the Irish hierarchy (especially with Desmond Cardinal Connell of Dublin), imposed serious strains on a Church-state relationship. That relationship was already in flux thanks to the New Ireland: self-confident and, until recently, economically buoyant; socially progressive and culturally fertile; increasingly European in outlook, cosmopolitan in taste, and sensitive to an emerging plurality of faith and ethnicity in the major urban centres.

This New Ireland is also increasingly ill at ease with the *ancien régime*. There is an undisguised anti-clericalism among the intelligentsia and the journalists, a determination among the current generation of Irish youth to relegate religious practice entirely to the private sphere (when there is practice at all), and mounting disengagement with the official Church by large numbers of middle-aged and mainstream Catholics who have no intention of abandoning their faith or discontinuing participation in its sacramental life, but who have become restive and even militant in their view that the Church is incapable of speaking to the moral issues of the day with credibility. In the February 2010 issue of *The Furrow*, the former provincial of the Irish Jesuits, Gerry O'Hanlon, notes the post-conciliar malaise that afflicts contemporary Ireland and calls for an ecclesiological renewal that also entails a radical reconsidering of the way bishops are appointed:

> Sadly, for a multitude of reasons, the dream of the Second Vatican Council of a more collegial church, with active lay participation, and a balancing of the power of the papacy with the influence of local churches (episcopal conferences, informed by lay input), have for the most part not been realized. The dominant culture of our Church remains that of a dysfunctional, autocratic clericalism. Many women

Religious know this only too well. We have had in Ireland some small steps forward with, for example, the development of parish councils, but there has been little sense of urgency about this movement. Perhaps this has been due in no small part to what theologian Nicholas Lash has identified as the conflicting interpretations of Vatican II, the success of the Roman Curia in resisting reform and effectively ensuring that collegiality has yielded to a more entrenched centralization ... Now would also seem to be a good time to call into question the reality that certain narrow grounds of orthodoxy are a *sine qua non* of episcopal appointment at present, and to call for more transparent and accountable local, including lay, participation in the appointment of bishops. It's instructive to note that as recently as 1829, of 646 diocesan bishops in the Latin Church, only 24 had been appointed by the Pope: often we forget how new many of our 'traditions' are.

O'Hanlon's cautious yet still pointed criticism speaks to the majority feeling of many Irish Catholics – priests, religious and lay – that part of the present Irish crisis around clerical sex abuse is also an ecclesiological crisis. It is a crisis that is defined in terms of a centralized authority that has marginalized the progressive calls for meaningful lay participation – read: the Vatican – and an unimaginative or tepid leadership that appears disconnected from the faithful – read: the Irish episcopacy.

But if these concerns have bubbled to the top because of the current sex scandals, the ugly fact remains that it was an unholy alliance of state and Church that precipitated the breakdown. A Norbertine priest, Brendan Smyth, whose diabolical skills at sexual predation spanned years and accumulated an appalling toll in victims, managed for a time to avoid extradition from the North to the Republic because of collusion between some cabinet ministers and Church officials. When this story became public, outrage among the Irish citizenry on both sides of the border guaranteed that the long and cozy relationship between Church and state in Eire was now beginning its messy unravelling.

Writer and publisher Brendan McCarthy notes in his *Tablet* article "Against the Dying of the Light" (March 27, 2010) that in the aftermath of the Smyth Affair, "the late Cardinal Cahal Daly [Primate of All Ireland and Archbishop of Armagh] was booed on RTE's *Late Late Show*. If there was a moment that marked the end of deference in Irish Catholicism, this was it."

But for all the Church's astounding sins, no less a figure than the cultural theorist, novelist, memoirist and Marxist critic Terry Eagleton could still find grounds for thanks. In his *Reason, Faith, and Revolution: Reflections on the God Debate*, Eagleton strikes a note of grudging gratitude:

> The Catholic church is in such understandably bad odour in Ireland these days that people sometimes cross the street when they catch sight of a priest approaching. In the old days it was probably a landlord. Yet the cruelties and stupidities that the Irish church has perpetrated do not prevent me from recalling how, without it, generations of my own ancestors would have gone unschooled, unnursed, unconsoled, and unburied.

Sadly, the accomplishments of the past and the history of service are easily eclipsed by the outrages and infamies of the present. From Smyth to the papal letter to the Irish, from the public humiliation of the Church's premier bishop on a popular television program to calls for the resignation of the current primate, Seán Cardinal Brady, the Church in Ireland continues to wrestle with its past and to fret openly about its future.

No one has more emphatically, and at personal cost, pushed for this openness and embodied its chastened and heroic aspects better than Archbishop Diarmuid Martin, the fearless agent of reform in the very bowels of the structure. As he said to a packed Holy Thursday Mass in his Pro-Cathedral of St. Mary's in Dublin, "Shameful abuse took place with the Church of Christ. The response was hopelessly inadequate. I do not wish to give the impression that I want to go on forever hammering home a message of grief about the past, that I am obsessed with the past. Some ask me, 'Can we not leave all that aside now, proclaim closure and move on?' I cannot agree. There can be no overlooking the past."

Martin is not enmired in the past, nor is he given to a pathological obsession with it. Rather, he understands that for the Irish Church to heal as a *Church*, it must acknowledge its sins and dig deep for the healing, no matter how painful; initiate reforms to guarantee that the institutional abuses of the past do not happen again; seek reparation for the victims; bring to the light misjudgments and possible criminal behaviour of senior hierarchs, so that public accountability may be rendered; and identify the enemy where it lies: in the bosom of a Church that is ruthlessly committed to avoiding scandal at all costs, including the innocence of the young and vulnerable.

Martin, a savvy media prelate with extensive curial and international diplomatic experience, is committed to full disclosure – not because he wants to hamper the Church's ministry, but because he wants to recover its credibility.

To that end, he has co-operated with the media, resisted the temptation to excoriate reporters and journalists as the Antichrist, and as a bishop has accepted the crucial need to be transparent and to eschew the false collegiality proffered by a clerical culture of concealment. But Martin is also a leader whose behaviour is often fraught with contradictions. Although exacting and persistent in his calls for episcopal reckoning, he too frequently uses the media to communicate with his own priests. In other words, the oracular reformer and curial veteran intent on cleaning house has failed to demonstrate to his fellow clerics a personal embodiment of the high ideals for cooperation and shared decision-making he espouses. Still, if not always consistent, he is a bracing breath of fresh air in a sealed environment.

If it was a difficult time for Martin, Archbishop of Dublin, it was considerably more so for Ratzinger, Bishop of Rome. The letter to the Irish merely presaged a torrent of reactions and revelations that Pope Benedict could not have anticipated and that went some way to eclipse much that was insightful and sensitive in the pastoral letter.

Overshadowing the letter itself were allegations cropping up all over Europe in the late winter and early spring of 2010: allegations of clerical abuse and cover-ups in Italy, Germany, the Netherlands and Switzerland. Of special significance was the case of a priest from the

Essen diocese in Germany – Peter Hullermann – who had been admitted for treatment to a therapeutic centre in the Archdiocese of Munich while Ratzinger was archbishop. What did the future pope know about the Hullermann case? How informed was he about allegations that Hullermann had abused minors? Did Ratzinger personally authorize Hullermann's restoration to active ministry after his formal treatment by psychologists? Memos, meeting agendas and recollections by several archdiocesan curial officials compounded the confusion around the issue, especially when it became clear that the advice of the consulting psychiatrist, Dr. Werner Huth, was not heeded. The Vicar-General at the time, Msgr. Georg Grüber, has assumed full responsibility for the handling of the Hullermann case. Although the future pope did not emerge entirely unscathed by this new investigation – there are legal cases pending against Hullermann – it was clear that Ratzinger's involvement would have been quite removed and his knowledge of the particulars minimal or non-existent.

But before the Hullermann dust could settle, the case of one Father Lawrence Murphy of Wisconsin was unfolding with a vengeance. Murphy had been a chaplain at the St. John's School for the Deaf, where he is alleged to have molested some 200 students between 1950 to 1974. At least two archbishops of Milwaukee, William E. Cousins and Rembert Weakland, knew of his reputation and the existence of the accusations. Cousins arranged for a transfer for Murphy to another diocese, where he worked for an additional quarter of a century unsupervised. Weakland implored Rome to act by defrocking Murphy, although he was late in doing so and his overriding concern was for the reputation of the Church. Weakland knew of the rising anger among the many molested deaf, and feared that nothing other than a strong canonical censure – with the extreme sanction of reduction to the lay state – could assuage the anger and hurt of the victims. Otherwise, the Church would be open to charges of complicity and callousness. Although he made the request several times by letter and intervened personally while in Rome on *ad limina* visits, he never received a response from the then Cardinal Ratzinger.

In the end, Murphy was not defrocked and was allowed to die as a priest, as his passing was imminent and he had made a request to the Congregation for the Doctrine of the Faith to be granted this final leniency. Weakland said in an interview with *The New York Times* (March 25, 2010) that the evidence against Murphy "was so complete, and so extensive that I thought he should be reduced to the lay state, and also that that would bring a certain amount of peace in the deaf community." The year was 1998.

So why are these cases surfacing now? Undoubtedly, lawyers involved with the civil suits see this as an opportunity to maximize damage to the Vatican's reputation, generate public outrage over the abuses, win sympathy for their clients, and create a climate where Rome is on the defensive or in full retreat. If the pope himself can be implicated – directly or by insinuation – all the better. Precisely because Church leaders are now co-operating with the civil authorities, and because Freedom of Information legislation allows access to hitherto sensitive, off-limits data, it is not surprising as the suits escalate that controlled disclosures to the press have become a feature of the legal challenges.

What *is* surprising are the strategically orchestrated revelations and the fact that the supreme pontiff himself is becoming increasingly the target. Surprising because Benedict is the pope who has most firmly addressed the issue; in his 2005 Good Friday meditation, his reference to "filth in the church" was universally understood to refer to clerical child sex abuse. In addition, four years earlier he had been instrumental in persuading John Paul II to transfer to his office direct responsibility for dealing with these cases. And so the *motu proprio Sacramentorum Sanctitatis Tutela* confirmed Cardinal Ratzinger as the key figure in the Church for dealing with a disturbing rise in cases involving sexually exploitative clerics. It was becoming increasingly clear to Ratzinger, if not the pope, that this was no North American phenomenon.

More importantly, as discussed in Chapter Three, Ratzinger was disturbed by the ongoing controversy surrounding the founder of the Legionaries of Christ, Marcial Maciel Degollado, a priest who exercised enormous influence in the Vatican, proved a formidable fundraiser, established universities, colleges, seminaries, and bought up property in the Holy Land at an astonishing rate. He also appeared to enjoy the special pleasure of John Paul II himself, who seemed disinclined to heed the volume of criticism and allegations of sexual abuse directed at Maciel. Much of the criticism was coming from former as well as current Legionaries; the veracity of their witness could not be discounted as anti-Catholic calumnies. Ratzinger pushed for a canonical investigation by his own Congregation in 2004.

No sooner was John Paul dead than Benedict censured Maciel in 2006 confining him to a life of penance and prayer and refusing him the right to celebrate Mass in public. And when the Maciel bubble finally burst – as it did – Ratzinger's suspicions were vindicated and his initiatives to curtail the influence of the Founder of the Legionaries of Christ and to scour some of what he addressed as filth was rightly applauded. However, it does raise concerns over John Paul II's puzzling inaction and defines to some degree the limitations of Ratzinger's ability to persuade John Paul as to the enormous gravity of morally errant priests and their impact on the Church. This has been confirmed by an interview that Christoph Cardinal Schönborn, the Dominican Archbishop of Vienna, gave on Austrian state television. Schönborn, while defending Benedict against accusations of a cover-up, alluded to the Hans Hermann Groër case and testified personally to the difficulties Ratzinger had in making progress on a seemingly intractable matter that could and should have been resolved with dispatch.

Cardinal Groër – Schönborn's immediate predecessor – had been embroiled for years in an accusation that he had sexually abused a minor when he was a Benedictine abbot. Groër refused to respond to his detractors, neither acknowledging guilt nor defending himself. In time, as the publicity and outrage ratcheted up and the Austrian hierarchy found itself increasingly pitted against Groër and his few diminishing supporters, the Vatican, and John Paul in particular, waffled, hesitated and then finally moved when it was too late and significant damage had been inflicted on the Austrian Church.

In his interview, Schönborn, an intellectual who has worked with Ratzinger for decades, dramatically paused and said to his interlocutor,

> I am now going to tell you something which I have not said in public before. While Joseph Ratzinger had wanted the Groer affair investigated in the Vatican, the other part – the diplomatic party in the Secretariat of State who wanted to shove everything on to the media – prevented an investigation from taking place. I distinctly remember Ratzinger saying sadly afterwards, "The other party got its way."

Although Schönborn did not hesitate to break ranks with his fellow prelates in the Vatican's Secretariat of State in order to defend his close colleague, such a disclosure casts a serious light on those eager to protect one of their own and on their willingness to play the media card when it suited them. Schönborn would pay a price for his increasingly public criticism of Vatican officials. Summoned to Rome for a meeting with the pope, soon to be augmented by the presence of Tarcisio Cardinal Bertone and Angelo Cardinal Sodano, the current and the immediate past Secretary of State for the Vatican respectively, the Austrian cardinal received a dressing down for his indiscretion in remonstrating with another cardinal in public. The pontiff reasoned that such behaviour indirectly called into question the judgment of the pope himself, as all cardinals are his "creation." The point was made. A chastened Schönborn returned to Vienna. Sodano appeared vindicated. Benedict's moral authority, however, in the eyes of many, was further weakened. Schönborn's major crime: he spoke openly with the media. We will return to this point later in the chapter.

Indeed, "blame the media" has become a tired and counterproductive mantra not only for many in the episcopate and in the Vatican, but among their acolytes. For instance, Damian Thompson, Blogs Editor of the Telegraph Media Group in England – an author, Evelyn Waugh wannabe and ascerbic polemicist – has delighted in eviscerating the British qualities, *Telegraph* excepted, that have adopted a hypercritical stance towards the Vatican in general and Benedict in particular. *The Times* and its religion correspondent, Ruth Gledhill, are his special target. Although many of the key British publications seem to have been infected by a strain of papaphobia that blinds them from being vigorously objective in their coverage, this is not by any means universally the case, nor is it always consistently true of individual columnists, reporters and editors. Much coverage is both discriminating and fair. The same is true of the BBC, whose Catholic Director-General, Mark Thompson, is regularly at pains to demonstrate the Corporation's balanced approach to religious reportage. There are, naturally, many egregious cases where such balance is lacking – many of the *Panorama* documentaries on clerical sex abuse have been driven by a stridency of view that may befit the interests of an investigative unit, but they sacrifice historical context and theological nuance in the process – but it is generally true that an institutional bias does not exist. It serves the interests of the papaphilia crowd, however, to picture the pope as the mercilessly bludgeoned victim of a media conspiracy and, in the process, absolve the Vatican and the episcopate from their responsibilities of oversight and accountability.

Canada's priest-columnist Raymond J. de Souza, for example, used his *National Post* column of April 8, 2010, to question the validity of many of the working assumptions of *New York Times* reporter Laurie Goodstein in her coverage of Benedict's "association" with the Murphy case, and her reliance on attorney Jeffrey Anderson ("the most prolific contingency-fee lawyer in suing the Church"). But in the process, de Souza scored many points against the former Archbishop of Milwaukee, Rembert Weakland, shifting responsibility onto his shoulders and thereby deploying the weakest of rhetorical and logical arguments – the *argumentum ad hominem*: "the disgraced former archbishop," "the compromised former archbishop."

In other words, not satisfied with launching an appropriate query regarding the fairness of the *Times* reportage, de Souza chose to further discredit a liberal archbishop whose serious misjudgments and flaws have already been exposed – Weakland was compelled to buy off his former gay lover to avoid further blackmail – but whose legacy of extraordinary accomplishments does not deserve to be so easily erased. Weakland's wounded leadership does not merit the summary observation that Goodstein chose to ignore how "discredited Weakland was" because she wrote a flattering story of Weakland's autobiography and must have approved of his "longtime hostility to Pope Benedict." In other words, Goodstein's coverage of the Vatican is compromised by her partiality towards Weakland. This is a nasty surmise rather than a rigorous exercise in logic.

A number of leading metropolitans and curial prelates defended Benedict over and against what was seen as a carefully engineered attack on the credibility of the papacy and the integrity of the pope himself. Vincent Nichols of Westminster, Timothy Dolan of New York, George Pell of Sydney and Angelo Sodano, former Secretary of State and Dean of the College of Cardinals, in addition to many others, chose direct combat with the media and appeared to give credence to a conspiracy of some sort. Other bishops throughout the world chose the Holy Week ceremonies – particularly the Mass of the Holy Chrism – to support the pope *without* adopting a combative stance with the media and avoiding conspiracy theories entirely. Archbishop Thomas Collins of Toronto spoke of the priesthood and virtuousness. The official statement of the Canadian Conference of Catholic Bishops, signed by the President Pierre Morissette of Saint-Jérôme, pledged support for the Holy Father and expressed confidence that under his leadership "we will move forward from pain to healing." Significantly, the CCCB letter acknowledges the "unprecedented number of reports which claim that you have not responded properly to the problems of sexual abuse of minors" and recognizes that, on the contrary, Benedict's leadership has been strong and decisive. He refuses to castigate the media, ascribe conspiratorial motives to its investigations, or condemn outright its research. This more nuanced approach allows for a reasoned defense rather than the "circling the wagons" strategy employed by many others.

In sharp contrast with Sodano's blistering jeremiads against the media, suggesting plots of devious calculation and worse, Schönborn commented at a service in Vienna that he often felt that the Church was being treated unfairly but that is not the way to go:

Why above all is the Church being put in the pillory? Isn't there abuse elsewhere as well? Is that not being investigated or come to terms with? And then I have sorely been tempted to say, "Yes. The media doesn't like the Church! Perhaps there is even a conspiracy against it?" But then I feel in my heart that no, that isn't it. And even if it were true, the mirror that is being held up to us shows us something that makes abuse in the Church particularly serious. It defiles God's Holy Name.

Similarly, Walter Cardinal Kasper, President of the Pontifical Council for Promoting Christian Unity, told Bavarian Radio that it was the media's job to make things public and the Church's job to put its own house in order. Still, at the same time that Klaus Mertes, the Jesuit head-master of the prestigious Canisius College in Berlin, was apologizing to pupils who had been abused by priests, and identifying emphatically that the "real enemy is the silence, not the media who broke the silence and that we in the church are not victims of the media but rather responsible for the very silence that is a continuation of the abuse," Gerhard Müller, Bishop of Regensburg, was scolding the very same media for being nothing more than "silly geese who hiss and spit."

The Tablet – in a critical leader titled "A Church in Need of Scrutiny" – on April 3, 2010, pointedly reminded its readers that it was the media that first exposed this cancer eating away at our vital organs, and that to shoot the messenger was hardly a helpful way forward to a cure:

> while ecclesiastical and even civil authorities refused
> at first to listen to what the victims of sexual abuse

had to say, the only people to give them a hearing were in the media. If the voice of the victims seems unduly amplified now – and it is by no means easy to say how much volume is too much – this is some compensation for the silence that reigned before … It [the BBC] exposed the grave mistake made by Cormac Murphy Cardinal O'Connor (former Archbishop of Westminster) in one notorious case when he was Bishop of Arundel and Brighton, which he quickly admitted with deep regret. He did not blame the press, or claim a media conspiracy, and he eventually emerged with his reputation restored.

The key words – "did not blame the press, or claim a media conspiracy" – stand in marked contrast with the perception in various senior Church circles that the media will stop at nothing to defame the pope and bring down the Church, that the media is the host guard for the forces of secularism, moral relativism and anti-clericalism, which have as their satanic resolve the full discrediting of the Church and all that it represents. In light of the aggressive new atheism that has become fashionable and highly popular through its leading polemical exponents Richard Dawkins, Christopher Hitchens, Sam Harris and other lesser luminaries, and in light of the bad press attached to institutional religion because of jihadism and religious terrorism in India, Sri Lanka, Pakistan, the Middle East and among the former Russian satellites, it is not difficult to understand why the Church might see the media, if not as the enemy, certainly in service to the enemy.

And what is true of continental Europe and the Vatican is true of the United States and Canada as well.

Old names and controversies resurfaced. Accusations of episcopal impropriety appeared for the first time or reappeared with a twist. Defrocked and jailed priests such as Robert Trupia of Tuscon, Arizona, and Stephen Kiesle of Oakland, California, were back on the front burner as lawyers unearthed documentation that pointed to episcopal incompetence, huge legal costs and Vatican foot-dragging.

But it was the Canadian Bernard Prince who drew the sharpest attention. The one-time monsignor, former assistant general secretary of the Canadian Conference of Catholic Bishops and secretary-general of the Pontifical Society for the Evangelization of Peoples (*Propaganda Fide*), Prince was found guilty of molesting thirteen boys between 1964 and 1984. He was sentenced, incarcerated and, in May of 2009, formally laicized by Rome.

What prompted the public outcry was the release to the press of a letter to the papal nuncio, Carlo Curis, from Prince's bishop Joseph Windle of the Diocese of Pembroke, Ontario. In the letter, dated February 10, 1993, Windle implores the nuncio not to consider Prince for any ecclesiastical preferment, episcopal appointment or honorary decoration, as the ramifications of Prince's behaviour are greater than originally thought. Indeed, the isolated incident that the local authorities dealt with originally had now mushroomed, as various sources and sordid details were now surfacing, the veracity of which had yet to be established but "once a matter of this nature becomes public it has a tendency to escalate and ... it might become worse as events unfold."

Windle's concern for the Church's reputation is his priority; although he is not without sympathy for the victims, and one in particular, his overriding preoccupation is to safeguard the Church's public image and limit the damage caused by Prince's behaviour.

One passage in the letter is especially regrettable, as it conveys an ethnic caricaturing and condescending attitude that would ordinarily convey the impression that the author is manipulative and cynical. Windle notes that there is "one redeeming factor [in] that it would appear that the victims involved are of Polish descent and their respect for the priesthood and the Church has made them refrain from making these allegations public or laying a criminal charge against a priest. Had this happened elsewhere there would be every danger that charges would have been laid long ago with all the resultant scandal." If it were not, therefore, for the native piety of the Poles, the Church would suffer grievously.

By all accounts, Windle was a very kind and caring man, but already out of sync with the times and dangerously naive about the larger consequences of his decisions. It is not so much that Windle is calculating as that he is ill-equipped to handle the evolving crisis. He reminds the nuncio that several Ontario bishops are aware of the situation and consider that any ecclesiastical promotion for Prince "would have horrendous results and cause immeasurable harm." And he meant to the institutional Church. He was every inch the man of the Church, and therein lies the deeper problem.

Although many church officials have attacked the media for continuing to raise these "old cases," Father Thomas Patrick Doyle, a canonist and co-author of *Sex, Priests and Secret Codes: The Catholic Church's 2,000-year*

Paper Trail of Sexual Abuse remarked in *The Tablet* of April 3, 2010,

> No matter how "old" the case is, it is not a dossier of paper. It is a human being who was once an innocent, devout and trusting Catholic child who now, as an adult, still lives with the intense pain and spiritual isolation that the years cannot heal. The victims were pushed into the shadows back then, and today, in the middle of the debate, one wonders what has changed. They have suffered devastation and yet they are still relegated to the shadows by a Church obsessed with protecting its hierarchy.

Doyle does not pull his punches. He has a long history of conflict with the hierarchy – American, specifically – over the clerical sex abuse phenomenon. He initially worked closely with the bishops while attached to the Vatican embassy in Washington. He co-authored a report on the pending crisis in the mid-1980s with the priest-psychiatrist Michael Peterson and the civil lawyer F. Ray Mouton, then encountered a wall of resistance and denial that saw their report, variously called "the document" or "the Manual," permanently shelved by a nervous hierarchy. The American episcopate, although at one point open to the work done by Doyle, Peterson and Mouton, decided to opt for their own committee and for the development of a strategy of coping that would rely on their own counsel.

Not surprisingly, Doyle ran into difficulties when he proved both prophetic and obstreperous. Peterson died and Mouton turned to writing his novel, *Beyond Familiar Altars* ("a story of scandal and cover-up in the Catholic Church").

Still, the U.S. Church, if slow to respond to the escalating crisis in Massachusetts, Louisiana and California – to say nothing of the emerging problems in dioceses across the nation – did move in 2002 to write and approve *Promise to Protect, Pledge to Heal: A Charter for the Protection of Children and Young People*. They also established the Essential Norms for diocesan/eparchial policies dealing with allegations of sexual abuse of minors by priests and deacons. The key principles and procedures of the Charter included the creation of an Office for Child and Youth Protection, the publication of reports on the implementation of the Charter using independent compliance audits, the establishment of a National Review Board to assist in the implementation of diocesan applications of the objectives of the Charter, the placement of victims' assistance coordinators throughout the country, the use of local diocesan review boards to ensure episcopal adherence to the Charter, and the widespread creation of safe environment programs to help parents and those who work with the young.

In 2005, the bishops revised and reissued the Charter and the norms, strengthening their commitment to act "in a spirit of collegiality and fraternity," while respecting the legitimate and autonomous exercise of authority by the bishops themselves and their direct accountability to the Holy See.

Most notably, the U.S. bishops adopted a zero-tolerance policy whereby "even a single act of sexual abuse by a priest or deacon [once] admitted or ... established after an appropriate process in accord with canon law ... will be removed permanently from ecclesiastical ministry, not excluding dismissal from the clerical state."

This was a controversial pledge on behalf of the U.S. Episcopal Conference that raised alarm bells in various Vatican quarters at first. It was seen as too severe and precipitous, but given the ecclesial reality on the ground, the zero-tolerance policy remains firmly in place.

In Britain, the Catholic Bishops' Conference of England and Wales – following the rising concern around child abuse – received a working party report in 1994 called *Child Abuse: Pastoral and Procedural Guidelines*, with another report appearing in 1996 titled *Healing the Wound of Child Sexual Abuse*. Then, in 2001 the Lord Nolan Report, *A Programme for Action*, was published. An extraordinarily thorough report that established a framework for best practices and prevention, the Nolan Report made 83 recommendations. Its express and overriding purpose was to help to "bring about a culture of vigilance where every single adult member of the Church consciously and pro-actively takes responsibility for creating a safe environment for children and young people. Our recommendations are not a substitute for this but we hope will be an impetus towards such an achievement."

When Cormac Murphy-O'Connor invited Lord Nolan to chair an independent committee to carry out a thorough review of child protection in the Catholic Church of England and Wales, he was determined that it be seen as an arm's-length body reporting to him but not subject to episcopal constraints. The composition of the committee itself reflects the Archbishop of Westminster's resolve that the body be diverse, professional, non-partisan, objective and broadly representative of the various strands and competencies of the British public: police officials, a psychiatrist, lawyers, social workers, child protection co-ordinator, clerics and civil service bureaucrats. In addition, there was gender balance and broad religious representations, with only four of the six members being Catholic. The cardinal was serious. This would be a commission one would be obligated to listen to, whose authority and composition was transparent, and whose mandate was unambiguous. This was not an exercise in spin doctoring; it was an exercise in pastoral leadership.

In addition, to ensure that *A Programme for Action* would not be shelved in some chancery office, Cardinal Murphy-O'Connor, in accordance with one of the recommendations, determined that a review be conducted five years after its adoption in order to ascertain how much progress had been made in implementing the recommendations. To that end, he established the Cumberlege Commission in 2006. Chaired by Baroness Cumberlege, with the Baroness Butler-Sloss as Vice-Chair – and with a membership that covered all the pertinent statutory and voluntary sectors, including several Catholic Church members with relevant theological and ecclesiastical expertise – the commission has produced its own reports over the years. These reports invigilated the progress in implementation, made recommendations, assessed areas of strength and deficiency, and provided timely updates.

In Canada, as has been already noted, the Conference of Catholic Bishops' document *From Pain to Hope* has itself been subject to review and revalidation. And yet, following the Windle and Prince revelations, it became apparent that there is no national body conducting a diocese-by-diocese annual assessment of compliance, nor a central office accumulating relevant data that would allow the bishops to compare dioceses. The argument advanced by the Secretariat in Ottawa, that the Conference does not have the financial resources to undertake such comprehensive actions (although undoubtedly true, given the economic constrictions imposed by the downsizing of the national office), seriously weakens the Canadian episcopate's resolve to be seen as serious about the recommendations that emanated from a report that was prophetic in content, morally urgent in tone, and a template for national conferences around the world. The English and American commissions and reports, although later than the Canadian in genesis, enjoy greater institutional commitment, extensive financial underwriting and public pledges of annual review and compliance. In January 2008, however, the CCCB did, under its then president James Weisgerber, Archbishop of Winnipeg, issue *Orientations*. This document was designed to "repeat, clarify and reinforce the recommendations in *From Pain to Hope* which has been an indispensable reference."

Orientations was conceived of as a handbook "to assist Catholic dioceses in Canada in updating their diocesan protocols for the prevention of sexual abuse," but at the same time painstakingly noted that each bishop remains autonomous. It excluded any mention of establishing a national registry, a process for compiling annual statistics, or an invigilating agency that would review local diocesan adherence to its own protocols and compare its success with other Canadian dioceses.

Other episcopal conferences around the world have either begun or recently ratified new procedures for reporting abuse to Church and civil authorities, and in the process conducting a review of their own past practices, creating channels of contact for victims, revisiting past cases that were handled in-house, and committing to co-operation with their respective civil authorities. Such places include Switzerland, Germany, Denmark and India. Even the Vatican has undertaken to remind the universal episcopate, through its Spring 2010 posting of those guidelines to be followed when dealing with allegations of abuse, that no circumventing of the civil law requirements in their respective jurisdictions should occur. As Lord Nolan noted when listing those essential qualities necessary for either restoring or retaining public confidence in the church authorities – "selflessness, integrity, objectivity, accountability, openness, honesty and leadership" – these qualities are principles of public life and are at heart Gospel principles.

Although the elaboration and application of procedures, protocols and sanctions by various episcopal conferences are now becoming the norm, bishops in previous decades were not entirely inactive in finding ways to cope with clergy accused of abuse. Prior to the explosion of cases beginning in the 1980s, past practice consisted in sending erring clergy to centres for spiritual and psychological rehabilitation, such as the "penitentiary" in Stroud, England (so mercilessly caricatured in Jim McGreevey's film *Priest*); the Institute for Living in Hartford, Connecticut; the Southdown Institute in Aurora, Ontario; St. Luke's Institute in Maryland; as well as to the various therapy centres run by such congregations as the priests of the Society of the Holy Paraclete in Sante Fe, New Mexico, who specialized in the treatment of clergy.

In other words, things actually were done. Although some bishops were undoubtedly remiss in not addressing the problem at all, and merely moving suspected clerics to new pastoral areas, suppressing all incriminating data, intimidating victims and their parents, and putting all the relevant files under an inviolable seal of confidentiality, most bishops behaved more honourably and responsibly. They relied on mental health professionals – psychiatrists, clinical psychologists, therapists and others – to guide their actions. They sent their men away for treatment. And then they restored them to active ministry when they received professional assurances that their abusing clergy were "cured."

In this they were naive. Akin to the vast majority in society, including many of the professionals they had consulted, they did not realize the incurability of pedophilia, failed to grasp the larger consequences of recidivism, were ignorant of the finer distinctions around psychosexual disorders (for instance, that pedophiles are interested in pre-pubescent children, under age 13, and should be distinguished from ephebophiles, who are interested in post-pubescent teenagers). Also, they assumed that with a declared intention for reform, a contrite attitude, appropriate remorse and spiritual humility, what was wrong could in time be righted.

In some instances, the clergy who returned to ministry were confined to places with restricted access to children and their behaviour was monitored, but in the vast majority of cases they were taken at their word, shuffled around until new suspicions surfaced, and not brought to the attention of the police. It was still seen as an in-house matter to be solved using in-house resources.

Scandal was to be avoided at all costs; the good of the institution was the highest good.

The number of cases has crested – at least in North America – with the preponderance of instances occurring between 1965 and 1980. Yet the decline in actual allegations of abuse has neither diminished the intensity of the crisis nor resulted in restoring confidence among Catholics and non-Catholics alike that the matter has been wisely and conclusively handled.

Besides seeking the counsel of health professionals, the bishops also had their lawyers advising them. This advice led them in a direction that often radically contradicted their most basic pastoral instincts. Rather than seeing the victims and their families as the primary beneficiaries of their attention and compassion, the bishops were required to see them as potential litigants and adversaries. The financial well-being of the diocese and all its good works could be imperilled by an overly conciliatory approach. Any admission of liability or culpability, no matter how oblique, could jeopardize the defense of the diocese in a court of law.

Handicapped by the professionals, trained to avoid scandal at all costs, besieged by an increasingly aggressive media that they had no skill in countering or deftly facilitating, the bishops found themselves increasingly at sea. Priests questioned their bishops' loyalty to them. The laity became intolerant of lame excuses and evasions. And Rome itself was beset by a wave of criticism with few recent parallels.

Rather surprisingly, those voices that should have been most heeded – the spiritual writers – have been recently neglected in the heat of battle. And yet their reflections are the most germane, biblically and historically sound, and sapiential.

The past Master of the Order of Preachers, Timothy Radcliffe, has not been shy in condemning the abuses of leadership, the betrayal of clerics and the sins of the cloth. But he has also secured these convictions within the context of a mature faith and a credible ecclesiology. In "Should I Stay or Should I Go? Clerical-abuse Scandal," published in *The Tablet* of April 10, 2010, he wrote,

> I am not a Catholic because our Church is the best, or even because I like Catholicism. I do love much about my Church but there are aspects of it which I dislike … From the beginning and throughout history, Peter has often been a wobbly rock, a source of scandal, corrupt, and yet this is the one – and his successors – whose task is to hold us together so that we may witness to Christ's defeat on Easter Day of sin's power to divide. And so the Church is stuck with me whatever happens. We may be embarrassed to admit that we are Catholics, but Jesus kept shameful company from the beginning.

Indeed we are embarrassed, shamed, humiliated, but as the spiritual writer and Oblate priest Ron Rolheiser observed at an earlier phase in the crisis in "On Carrying a Scandal Biblically," an address he gave at St. Jerome's University in Waterloo, Ontario,

> humiliation leads to humility. This is a moment of purification for the church. Granted the rest of the culture is also guilty, but, for too long, we falsely enjoyed clerical privilege. The chickens have come home to roost. Now we are being pruned, humbled, and brought back to where we're supposed to be, with

the poor, the outcasts. That's where we are meant to be. Jesus resisted all power other than moral power. Too often we bought into that power. Today the Body of Christ is not just being humbled, it's being humiliated and we have the chance to come to humility through that. This is an important grace-opportunity for all of us inside the church. Biblically, it's our Agony in the Garden.

Barry Craig, an Anglican priest and Vice-President Academic of St. Thomas University in Fredericton, New Brunswick, reminded Christians that identifying too closely with the old dispensation blinds us to the excesses of power, the corrosiveness of institutional pride and the spiritually lethal resistance to transformation. In his 2009 Saint John Advent Lecture, "No Longer at Ease Here in the Old Dispensation," he remarked that

in our time the church is beset on every side. It is more difficult to trust the institution and more difficult to believe. But I wonder if this is altogether a bad thing. When the church is filled with confidence, when it has a sense of its power, it is invariably set for a fall. The Body of Christ, the Bride of Christ, surely cannot clothe itself in *less* humility than Christ himself. Think of Christ in John's Gospel washing his disciples' feet; think of Christ before Pilate. Then think of our shock when the world reviles us or think of our surprise when we are humiliated because of the failings of our institutional church. *Why* are we shocked? *Why* are we surprised?

But shocked we are.

And that is so largely because humility, frailty and vulnerability are not qualities we have been instructed to see or even value in our Church.

But that has changed. Irrevocably.

7

The Struggle for Narrative: The Language of Apology

n June of 2010, Lord Saville, a British High Court judge, released his report into what actually happened on January 30, 1972, in the Bogside area of Londonderry, Northern Ireland. Fourteen people died that day, shot by British paratroopers, in what quickly became known as Bloody Sunday. This event marked the beginnings of the so-called Troubles. Lord Saville's 12-year inquiry, with testimony from 900 witnesses and at a cost of $300 million, was a relief to the victims' families, and the cause of an immediate public apology on the part of British Prime Minister, David Cameron. While not intending to be, the Saville inquiry is an indicator of just how difficult determining the truth might be, and how costly an exercise. It is perhaps even an object lesson in when and how to come clean on a scandal.

There are numerous approaches to the sexual abuse crisis. One of the most complicated – and perhaps the most necessary – is the casting of the story in a form that resonates with Catholics and the world at large. This is about more than the spin we talked about earlier. This is about the complex issue of the apology.

Expressing contrition, confessing a wrong, seeking forgiveness and doing penance is at the heart of the Catholic experience, both in its sacramental life and in its approach to moral living. The individual phenomenon is true as a lived experience.

Institutional apology is a different matter all together. A key difficulty is keeping track of what is being apologized for and understanding what flows from an apology. In this fraught 'age of apology,' this is not a simple proposition. It becomes even more complex when we acknowledge that apologies in real time need to be accepted. They are often held up to judgment in terms of adequacy, integrity, sincerity and continuity. These complex factors are by no means unique to the problem facing the Church, but bedevil all institutions.

Perhaps adding to the complexity of the apology conundrum, especially for the Church, is the issue of context. Consider this thought expressed by John Paul II in a letter to the U.S. Bishops in 1993 dealing with the efforts of the Bishops to confront Clerical Sexual Abuse:

> While acknowledging the right to due freedom of information, one cannot acquiesce in treating moral evil as an occasion for sensationalism. Public opinion often feeds on sensationalism and the mass media play a particular role therein. In fact, the search for sensationalism leads to the loss of something, which is essential to the morality of society. Harm is done

to the fundamental right of individuals not to be easily exposed to the ridicule of public opinion; even more, a distorted image of human life is created. Moreover, by making a moral offense the object of sensationalism, without reference to the dignity of human conscience, one acts in a direction which is in fact opposed to the pursuit of the moral good. There is already sufficient proof that the prevalence of violence and impropriety in the mass media has become a source of scandal. Evil can indeed be sensational, but the sensationalism surrounding it is always dangerous for morality.

*

Without doubt it was the scandal of the fall of 2009. The keepers of the faith, stern in their conviction that they knew the truth, that their behaviour was beyond reproach, insisted that the critics were know-nothings with a clear ideological agenda. It was a battle of wills and world views. At stake was nothing short of the future of humanity.

There were rumours, of course, that secret documents existed. If uncovered, they would show once and for all that key members of the leadership had manipulated facts, hidden excesses and engaged in lies and subterfuge to maintain power and silence critics. Critics believed that the rot, hubris and indifference to real and potential harm had spread throughout. The only true solution was to level everything and begin again. The true faithful saw a vast conspiracy arrayed before evident truth. They blamed the media for engaging in character assassination and conscious manipulation of fact and opinion to serve their own agenda. On both sides, the volume of denunciation, defensiveness, truth assertion and name-calling was nearly deafening.

Then, in November, documents surfaced detailing cover-ups, manipulation, truth twisting, plots to silence dissenters, and corrupt politicians and members of the media. Recriminations and apologies were immediate. Key members of the establishment insisted that errors on the part of the few were being blown out of proportion, and that even if some individuals had abused their positions, it did not affect the foundational truth. But in the disclaimers and pleas for forgiveness lay a tone of desperation, a sense that the tide had turned. The ground had shifted and something much more fundamental than a token apology was necessary if all was not to be lost.

But in fact all was lost, at least for the moment.

The December United Nations meeting on climate change in Copenhagen, which was tasked with bringing in a new accord that was more powerful than the Kyoto Accord, more attuned to the pressing need to avert global catastrophe, lost all necessary momentum when 'Climategate,' as it was quickly labelled by a lazy media, burst into the open. Key documents from the Climate Research Unit at the University of East Anglia had been hacked by still unknown individuals and released *en masse* to climate change deniers and the media. Leading figures in the world of climate change science were revealed to be superior, defensive individuals not above threatening all and sundry while at the same time engaging in behaviour that appeared for a time to consist of manipulating facts and fudging records. It was a serious blow to the idea of trying to curb human-generated global warming. No new accord was reached in Denmark. By June of 2010, there was insufficient political will left to even put climate change on the agenda of a meeting of world leaders in Toronto.

'Climategate' was and is an object lesson in how truths can quickly lose their hold on the hearts and minds of millions. More importantly, it was and is an object lesson in the importance of shaping narratives, as opposed to having a narrative shaped by one's critics, enemies or even – especially – one's friends.

It may be the ultimate irony of the Year of the Priest that it was *New Scientist* magazine that carried a major essay offering advice to the Catholic Church on how it might get out of the serious trouble it found itself in.

Of course, the famously anti-religious publication hadn't intended to offer such advice to the Church when it published an essay by Bob Ward, policy and communications director of The Grantham Research Institute on Climate Change and the Environment at the London School of Economics. What the author and the magazine set out to do was advise climate scientists, a group the magazine supports and is fond of, on how they might best get out of the turmoil created by the events of 2009 and the early months of 2010.

Largely basing the essay, and by extension the advice, on Leslie Gaines-Ross' *Corporate Reputation: 12 Steps to Safeguarding and Recovering Reputation*, Ward stressed three key actions that the leaders of any organization and institution should follow when faced with a crisis of reputation. In order, the necessary steps included "take the heat – leader first," "communicate tirelessly," and finally "don't underestimate your critics and competitors." As we will see, all of this is easier said than done. And arguably the Church has failed in all three respects, but obviously such a conclusion needs to be qualified. The Church is a large and varied institution and, as noted elsewhere, efforts on the part of different sections of the universal Church have been more or less successful.

The ultimate irony of the Year of the Priest has to be that the Church and climate change science faced shame, denigration and possible fatal blows in terms of trust and respect head on. What both shared as 2010 wound down were serious questions and doubts about whether either institution would be able to regain the import and leadership role it once played in its respective spheres. Equally serious were questions about their survival.

There are clear and important distinctions to be drawn between the Church and the practitioners of climate change science. For the moment, consider that both make serious claims to being seized with the truth, and that sins, misdeeds and even crimes by individuals cast doubt on truth claims. It is not just the Church's traditional enemies who see the story of the sex abuse scandal as evidence of hypocrisy and falsehood. The faithful are troubled, bewildered and occasionally be-reft of a way through this crisis that leaves faith intact, not to mention adherence to the institution. Serious theologians, deeply loyal believers and ordinary, trusting individuals are wrestling with the moral, human, insti-tutional and religious implications of the abuse scandal. Following the advice of 'reputation managers' may not be of sufficient help, but it won't be of much harm, either. In a world where people are as familiar with the tropes of advertising and public relations as they are with the volumes of The Great Books series, it isn't necessary to believe everything about message management. But it is dangerous to reject the possibility.

In April of 2010, an Ipsos Reid poll startled the world. According to a survey conducted in the winter by Ipsos, one of Canada's largest and most respected pollsters, 8 percent of Canadians, or two million people, "personally know someone sexually assaulted by a Roman Catholic priest." This astounding figure made national and international headlines. As Kevin Newman, host of Global TV's national news program, reported, the poll, commissioned by Global, "hints at just how widespread the problem of pedophilia may be."

"Two million people is a shocking number," said John Wright, senior vice president of Ipsos Reid, according to the *Regina Post-Leader*. "This is not something that can evade scrutiny."

"If we were experiencing H1N1 tomorrow with two million people, we would in fact shut down this country, because it would be a calamity," he told Global National. "We're dealing with what appears to be an epidemic."

In addition, the poll revealed that 58 percent of all respondents and 54 percent of those who self identified as Catholic put much of the blame for the crisis on the shoulders of Pope Benedict XVI, believing that he "perpetuated a climate of silence and cover-up around pedophile and peephole priests."

The Ipsos Reid poll or, we should say, the *reporting* of the Ipsos Reid poll, although it is ultimately about Canada and Canadians, speaks to the Church's difficulties in Ireland, in the United States, in Europe and in fact everywhere the Roman Catholic Church is present.

Numerous issues are raised by the poll, not the least of which was the rhetoric contained in the commentary on the poll by Ipsos Reid's John Wright. Words like "calamity" and "epidemic" and comparisons with deadly diseases are loaded terms. Perhaps they are used intentionally to hype a provocative survey. Using hyperbole and applying torque are to pollsters and the media what oxygen is to trees and water to life. The meaning of these terms is inescapable: the Church and its conduct are a plague that in other circumstances would demand drastic measures. That the sex abuse crisis demands action is without doubt, but proportion is necessary in both understanding the problem and responding to the problem.

One could say that the entire poll suffered from irremediable problems. Such a proposition was put forward by Reginald Bibby, Canada's pre-eminent sociologist on religion and a scholar with decades of experience in polling on matters of religion. In an essay published in the *Edmonton Journal*, Bibby asserted that while he had "no pro-Catholic axe to grind," and is not a Catholic himself, it was clear that the poll and the spin around the poll created a sensation that was not in " the best interest of everyone," especially given the "hyperbole on the part of pollsters who should know better." He then went on to characterize the poll as needing to be described as "inaccurate and unnecessarily inflammatory." He spent the rest of his essay trashing the methodology of the poll, the design of the questions asked, and the confusion caused by terms such as "awareness" and "incidence." He used a couple of illustrations to show the weaknesses of the poll.

Suppose, for example, that Ipsos-Reid had asked Canadians, "Do you have family members, friends, or acquaintances who have been divorced?" I'd venture to say that the question would have resulted in as many as 90 per cent of people across the country saying, "Yes." Contrast this to the number of people who have personally been divorced – my own latest national survey shows this figure is probably around 15 per cent.

The first question asks individuals about the people they know – and who doesn't know someone who has been divorced? The other asks individuals about their own experiences. Awareness does not equal incidence. Both are important. But obviously they are two very different things.

Take teenage suicide as another example. If one is to equate awareness with an epidemic, here's a major one: our latest national youth survey has found that about one in three teenagers has a close friend who has attempted suicide. Does that mean that one in three – or as many as one million Canadian teens – have tried to take their lives? Of course not. In one school of 1,000 students, for example, teenagers may have two or three people in mind – very serious, of course, but hardly an epidemic.

He also expressed incredulity about whether many or any Canadians possessed sufficient knowledge to make a judgment on what culpability, if any, was borne by the pope:

How on earth do Canadians have the inside scoop on whether or not the Pope has been part of the alleged scandal? A follow up question to the effect of

"On what are you basing your opinion?" may have been extremely telling. Obviously, most Canadians who offered a take were simply offering views based on information they have received from media and acquaintances. In short, the poll doesn't tell us very much – beyond Canadian conjecture.

The Canadian Conference of Catholic Bishops also responded to the Ipsos Reid poll. It took a decidedly different tack and emphasized what they saw as the positives to be drawn from the results. The fact that the younger the person polled, the less likely they were to assert that they knew someone abused by a priest, led the bishops to conclude that the efforts on the part of the CCCB to deal with the abuse problem were working. They also sided with the sense of concern the Canadian public seemed to be exhibiting, and stated that the bishops shared that concern. And they targeted an aspect of the poll ignored by Bibby: "A cursory reading of the results could lead one to conclude that the Catholic Church has a bigger problem with the issue of sexual abuse than any other segment of society. This is incorrect. Experts say that there is no data to support such a claim at all."

Arguing over poll results can be a dangerous undertaking. On the one hand, it is hard to let pass without comment something you know or believe to be wrong. The Canadian Catholic bishops are right in observing that sexual abuse is not confined to priests. They aren't the first or only national church to make this claim or voice this argument. But motes and planks aside, it must be admitted that polls measure beliefs, and that the relationship between truths and beliefs, especially in polling, is complicated. Asserting that the beliefs of the poll respondents are wrong has had little effect on the number of people who believe that Elvis lives.

Where everyone loses it in the war for reputation and the battle for public opinion dominance is in separating media accounts, narrative spins and reality. Postmodernists, but no one else, will assert that all realities are constructs and that the search for truth is futile and ultimately bogus. The rest of us actually believe that there is truth somewhere, but as we saw in the discussion about spin, sorting out truth can be difficult. Yet no one expects that truth might be as difficult to find as is the case in the matter of the Ipsos Reid poll on priests, pedophiles and abuse.

This is not just a matter of semantics, a bad 21st-century play on the attribution to Pontius Pilate, "What is truth?" We both have truths. Are mine the same as yours? Truth does matter. It matters in justice, punishment, redemption and taking the right corrective actions.

At the beginning of June 2010, at a conclave of nearly 15,000 priests in Vatican City, Pope Benedict XVI spoke out on the nature of the priest, the idea of celibacy and the litany of abuse tales that had so dramatically marked the entire year. The coverage of the papal address paid much attention to what was described as the pope's apology and his plea for forgiveness. What makes this issue special or worthy of note is that it was not the first time the pope had acknowledged the abuse crisis, apologized or asked for forgiveness. What matters is not when the media or the public pays attention so much as *why*.

As we will see, the papal address at the conclusion of the Year of the Priest proved to be a game changer; it was not a given that it would do so. Simply consider what happened when regrets, recriminations or apologies were uttered in the case of Bishop Lahey, for the abuse in Ireland and with respect to the horror of the residential schools in Canada. A more striking case study for 'relationship managers' is hard to imagine, if for no other reason than because the three cases are of such difference in magnitude, response and reaction.

There may be no more tragic, or complex, story of abuse than the story of Canada's residential school experience. In the mid-19th-century, the British and nascent Canadian governments were intent on dealing with the Aboriginal peoples of Canada through a policy of assimilation. This policy was the height of progressive and Church thinking at the time. People believed that Aboriginal peoples should be, as a matter of justice, integrated into the emerging industrial economy. This would be accomplished over time and through the schooling and the fostering of 'civilized behaviour' and Christianization.

For a century and a half, Aboriginal children were forcibly removed from family and community and sent to a system of schools, called residential schools, which were operated by Canada's major churches on behalf of the federal government. Nearly 70 percent of these schools were operated by religious orders and organizations affiliated with the Catholic Church; the rest were run by the United Church and Anglican Church of Canada.

The records are scattered and incomplete, but the agreed upon facts suggest that the schools operated for 150 years and took in at least 150,000 Aboriginal children. All of the numbers in the residential schools story are estimates offered by different groups, some with clear agendas. Part of the mandate of the Truth and Reconciliation Commission is to try and make real these 'facts.' Some historians argue that as many as 50,000 of these students died as a result of inadequate food and shelter, poor health and infectious disease. Some claim that thousands of others were sexually and physically abused by the people in charge of the schools, often clerics and ministers. And, in hindsight, it is admitted that every student suffered from emotional and cultural abuse through the simple fact of being taken from family and community and forced to endure a process calculated to "kill the Indian in the child,' in the words of one early 20th-century bureaucrat responsible for administering the program on the part of the Canadian government.

The last of the schools was closed as recently as 1996. But by the early 1990s a small group of self de-scribed 'residential school survivors' had started a class action suit against the Government of Canada and all the churches involved in the residential schools program. By 2007, there were thousands of claimants in the suit. A settlement involving all the parties was reached. It included compensation, a public apology on the part of the government and the establishment of a Truth and Reconciliation Commission. The Commission's task was to document the history of the schools and begin the process of reconciling Canada's Aboriginal peoples, the churches and the Canadian population in general.

The compensation flowed, though inevitably there are continuing arguments about adequacy, lawyer fees and eligibility. Clearly, this is still a very live issue. Apologies were issued, on at least three occasions, by both Liberal and Conservative governments: inside the House of Commons and in statements and addresses. Each time there were arguments from some about adequacy and sincerity as well as critical questions about the sufficiency of words. Ironically, at the same time as the Truth and Reconciliation Commission was embarking on its public events, another issue, thought to have been settled, resurfaced.

In July of 2010, representatives of Canada's Chinese Community went public with a complaint that the apology and compensation issued in 2006 for the "Head Tax" was insufficient. (The "Head Tax" was in place in Canada from 1885 to 1923. All Chinese immigrants to Canada were charged a fee for the 'privilege' of coming to Canada to take on some of the most onerous and dangerous jobs around.)

The apology was to the Chinese community. The compensation, $20,000, was paid to individuals who had paid the tax or to their surviving spouses. Members of the Head Tax Families Society of Canada, in a press conference in Vancouver, complained that the children and descendants of people who had paid the tax were not compensated, and that those who had already died gained nothing from the apology. Sid Tan, the grandson of a "head tax" payer, insisted, "The apology was not as meaningful to us as it was to other [Chinese families]. The federal government left out a large chunk of people and you have to find some way you can meaningfully provide redress for them."

Apologies are complicated, separate from redress and a continual source of controversy and acrimony. The Catholic Church knows this all too well.

Most of the Catholic organizations involved with the residential schools (if these organizations still existed), the Canadian Conference of Catholic Bishops (CCCB), as well as numerous individual bishops, priests, nuns and lay people, have tendered apologies, made acts of contrition and expressed seemingly true and sincere wishes for healing, forgiveness and moving forward.

On its website, the CCCB describes the official Canadian Church response to the residential schools situation, noting that "various types of abuse experienced at some residential schools have moved us to a profound examination of conscience as a Church." The CCCB also observes in its account of the residential schools experience that

> The Catholic community in Canada has a decentralized structure. Each Diocesan Bishop is autonomous in his diocese and, although relating to the Canadian Conference of Catholic Bishops, is not responsible to it.

> Approximately 16 out of 70 Catholic dioceses in Canada were associated with the former Indian Residential Schools, in addition to about three dozen religious communities. Each diocese and religious community is legally responsible for its own actions. The Catholic Church as a whole was not associated with the Residential Schools, nor was the Canadian Conference of Catholic Bishops.

These are the reasons why an apology on Residential Schools has not been made by the Canadian Conference of Catholic Bishops or in the name of the Catholic Church in Canada.

The Missionary Oblates of Mary Immaculate, the religious community that ran many of the schools, offered the most complete of apologies for any abuse committed by members of the order and its role in the overall abusive nature of residential schools. On July 24, 1991, Doug Crosby, OMI, then president of the Oblate Conference of Canada, spoke to an assembly of nearly 20,000 Aboriginal people on a traditional pilgrimage to Lac Ste. Anne in Alberta. He said,

> We apologize for the part we played in the cultural, ethnic, linguistic and religious imperialism that was part of the European mentality and, in a particular way, for the instances of physical and sexual abuse that occurred in these schools. We recognize that in spite of the good that came of them, the residential schools have caused pain to so many. For these trespasses we wish to voice today our deepest sorrow and we ask your forgiveness and understanding. We hope that we can make up for it by being part of the healing process wherever necessary.

The pope, meanwhile, has never issued an apology. Benedict XVI came close in 2009 when, after a private meeting with residential school survivors, the Vatican issued the following statement:

> Given the sufferings that some indigenous children experienced in the Canadian residential school system, the Holy Father expressed his sorrow at the

anguish caused by the deplorable conduct of some members of the church and he offered his sympathy and prayerful solidarity. His Holiness emphasized that acts of abuse cannot be tolerated in society.

In June of 2010, the Truth and Reconciliation Commission, led by Justice Murray Sinclair, with the assistance of fellow commissioners Marie Wilson and Chief Wilton Littlechild, held its first national event at the Forks in Winnipeg, Manitoba. Thousands of survivors of the school system, as well as descendants of those who have died, came together for four days to take part in healing ceremonies, receive more public apologies and offer witness to the experience. In many respects, the occasion was positive and optimistic. But there were also indications that despite the acknowledged apology for past wrongs, the story was far from over.

Talk increasingly turned to questions of identifying particular individuals as abusers, selecting institutions as possible targets of criminal and civil proceedings, seeking new forms of compensation and demanding new and increasingly complex forms of apology. It soon became clear that apologies may never be sufficient unto themselves. This is especially the case when apologies are qualified or deemed difficult because of complex organizational relations.

Consider Archbishop Anthony Mancini, Archbishop of the Diocese of Halifax. He was the man who had to step in when the charges against Bishop Lahey became known. Mancini was quick off the mark to express the sorrow and confusion everyone was experiencing, reassuring the parties to the ground-breaking sexual abuse settlement that Bishop Lahey had negotiated days before his sudden resignation, and describing a way forward.

In a public statement issued upon news of the arrest and charges of Bishop Lahey, Archbishop Mancini said,

> I have come to be with you in the midst of this sadness, pain and anxiety. I come with what I have, that is, my care and my concern. It is in this sense that I understand the shepherding role that I am asked to exercise here. Let me first speak to those victims of past sexual abuse and to all for whom this news rekindles past pain. These recent revelations take on the character of victimization. I wish it were not so. This is not what our community of faith is supposed to be about. We have already stated that this new reality will not undo the settlement with victims of sexual abuse that has been approved. I am well aware that everyone is in shock. I am concerned with all who are trying to find any meaning in this devastation. I do not have the solution to this problem, or the capacity to take away the pain, or the means to erase this tragedy. It may be that some would wish for a quick solution to the problems we are facing, but all that I know is that whatever the solution may be, it will be a matter of collaboration and faith, and we all must do our part.

> I have come today to meet with the priests and diocesan personnel, to reach out to all and to attempt to ensure that all will be cared for as best we can. It is important to recognize that we are standing in a place of brokenness and vulnerability right now.

In these very early days, we need to begin to look forward, not to escape this pain but to look at how we are being called to be the community of faith at this time. This calls for a great deal of hope, and belief that we do not do any of this alone. We are all in this together. I want to encourage the priests to gather with each other, that they may help one another to come to the greater appreciation that they are brothers in Christ, and so find the strength to continue in the ministry entrusted to them.

Also, I want to encourage parishioners to draw on each other's faith as you carry this painful burden and grieve for the losses that we are experiencing. If you can, bring this burden to the parish Eucharist, where we bring all our troubles. This is how we can continue to be the community of faith for and with one another in these times.

I am committed in spite of everything that has happened to try to help us all get to another place, more reflective of the Gospel we are about. This can be an opportunity for all of us to rediscover what it is to be the community of faith, to realize what the root of our faith really is, and how each of us helps to share the faith.

We are going through a very painful contemporary experience of the mystery of our Faith, which is all about Passion and Death yes, but it is also about the promise of Resurrection, without which we have no future. So I call on you to be hopeful because we believe in new life and new possibilities.

The language and approach of Archbishop Mancini is distinctly different from that used in the residential schools matter. Is it because the situations are different in degree when it comes to complexity, or is Archbishop Mancini simply a more subtle and astute communicator? The difference might be found in observing that Archbishop Mancini is not apologizing but rather is engaged in pastoral work of the highest kind. In the delicate politics of apologies, an apology may or may not be offered in the case of Raymond Lahey. It is part of the conundrum of apologies that where and why the apology comes is as tricky and critical as the content.

To some extent the issue is moot, though it is hard not to speculate about what a superb communicator might have said on the issue of the residential schools.

On the Irish abuse situation, which we look at in more detail elsewhere in this book, we get a much clearer sense of where apologies might be seen to have gone wrong. On March 21, 2010, the pope released a letter to the the Catholics of Ireland in which he wrote, "You have suffered grievously and I am truly sorry." He also admonished the Bishops of Ireland, "Serious mistakes were made. All this has seriously undermined your credibility."

Many people – most significantly the victims, but also the secular media, judged the pope's comments to be inadequate. Andrew Madden, a victim of abuse and part of One In Four, an Irish victims' abuse group, put it bluntly: "He didn't apologize for anything the church has done, only for the actions of pedophile priests. The Church's actions weren't just down to errors of judgment. This was a proactive covering up of the sexual abuse of children to avoid scandal for the church. Pope Benedict completely failed to own up to this."

A key difference between the problems faced by climate change scientists and the Roman Catholic Church is the question of time frame. Climate change as an idea has been around for less than 50 years; the Church has been in the world for two millennia. Climate change and the political sphere are at the initial stages of sorting out who does what and why; the Church has wrestled with its links to and relationship with secular society from day one. Time frames and history matter for our purposes only as much as we wrestle with how the Church incorporates both into truth telling, communication with the public, and remedial action.

At times, though, history and time frames can be barriers to communication. Distinctions on autonomy and relationships, the right ordering of responsibilities and power, the demands of justice and fairness towards the accused as well as the victims are reasonable, understandable, necessary and, in the world of apologies, beside the point. Apologies are about healing wounds, structuring narratives, making whole fractured relationships. Nuance and niceties are the stuff of lawsuits, legal agreements and organizational behaviour. Validity, necessity and legal correctness can and do stand in the way of truth, reconciliation and restoration.

This is a lesson learned too late by too many.

8

The Heart of the Matter

There is a prevailing myth – perhaps fostered by the Irish, but then again, perhaps not – that Irish Catholicism is exceptional. At the same time, it is seen as the model paradigm for exemplary Catholic life: after all, everything comes together to constitute one inclusive picture. This picture has been reinforced for decades, centuries even, by the Irish diaspora's romanticism, by Hollywood's love of caricature, and by Rome's close ties with a vocation-producing factory with few parallels. And so the sundering of this myth, the "undoing" of Catholic Ireland, invites close scrutiny in the light of the sex abuse scandals. The two events are inextricably linked and provide a cautionary warning.

It was the perfect tableau. All the players were there. The students couldn't have asked for a better panel.

It was the last week of class for 43 undergraduate American students from Sacred Heart University, Fairfield, Connecticut, who were enrolled in the university's "Theology and Native Irish Spirituality" semester course taught at An Díseart: An Institute of Culture and Spirituality in Dingle, Ireland. The students were to have four local eminences gather to respond to their frank questions about such things as the Celtic imagination, the Celtic mind, the Celtic tiger, and Ireland's national sport. They got that in spades.

But what the students also got – and it surprised many of those not from the Boston area – was an arrestingly frank demonstration of the four panellists' religious convictions. These 43 students were to discover the new Ireland.

The panel consisted of Eoin Moloney, founder of the website www.offtherecord.ie; Professor/Monsignor Pádraig Ó Fiannachta, teacher, writer, publisher and founder of An Díseart; Seán Pól ÓConchuir, Director of the Sacred Heart University Dingle campus; and T.P. Ó Conchúir, entrepreneur, publican, former politician and member of the Board of An Díseart.

Asked about religion in Ireland and their personal faith, the panellists spoke about the current upheaval, the deep sense of national shame, the unaddressed anger, and the unheard cry for accountability. They did not all sing from the same song sheet; there were marked differences.

Moloney spoke of his personal faith crisis, his unshakeable belief in God, his irregular appearances at church, and his deep loyalty to and affection for Ó Finnachta. The monsignor himself ruminated about the essentials of Christian faith, human weakness and spiritual resilience, all the while demonstrating those welcome personal qualities that continue to engage everyone he encounters. Seán Pól, the youngest of the four, deplored the hypocrisy in the Church, its political corruption and venality, doubted whether he would marry in the Church, and concluded with the now customary tribute to the monsignor. T.P., the most seasoned and world-weary of the lot, professed his continued attachment to the Church, publicly identified as a professed Catholic, and paid appropriate homage to the monsignor.

However, it was T.P.'s concluding story that provided the most striking note of the evening. Some ten years previous, he had gathered dozens of disenchanted women parishioners into his pub for a night of honest petitioning over the failures of local ecclesiastical leadership. These were highly articulate and committed women; T.P. was both moved and worried by what he had ignited. They were right to speak of *their* Church, but what would happen if, well, nothing happened? Now, a decade later, with problems of greater magnitude on the ecclesiastical shores, would these earlier expressions of concern morph into impotence or rage?

T.P. remained unsure of the future, but felt that lay people were now more mobilized than ever. If the church leadership failed to take serious heed of their frustration, Ireland could be lost to that very faith for which for centuries the nation was promoted as an exemplary witness.

One thing all three of the panellists agreed on – the monsignor proffered no opinion – was the need for the immediate resignations not only of auxiliary bishops, but ordinaries, and the primate himself – in short, all those in power during the periods covered by the Ryan and Murphy reports. Only the Archbishop of Dublin was to be spared.

What the students heard from the panellists they could also hear – almost nightly – in the local pubs, in bank lineups, among parents preparing their young families for First Communion and Confirmation, among secondary and university students enrolled in Irish institutions, in the marketplace, and among demoralized priests and religious.

Demands for Cardinal-Archbishop Séan Brady's resignation continued throughout the spring of 2010 with little abating. The demands came from many quarters: believing Catholics, media pundits, the intelligentsia and anticlericals. Brady said he would decide on his future at the time of Pentecost; at that time, he informed the Catholics of Ireland that although he would request assistance from Rome in the person of a bishop who may or may not have coadjutor status, he would serve his time as Archbishop and Primate of All Ireland and not offer his resignation to Rome.

Brady's decision immediately prompted expressions of disappointment. There was little in the way of a chorus of congregants clamouring for him to stay, although many of his fellow bishops no doubt breathed a sigh of relief. Perhaps now the pressure on them to resign as well would diminish. That certainly proved to be the case for two of Dublin's auxiliary bishops.

But Brady remains a special case. *Irish Times* columnist Vincent Browne put the dilemma both succinctly and nakedly in his May 19, 2010, column. In enjoining a vow of secrecy on two boys abused by the renegade Norbertine Brendan Smyth, and then tacitly allowing another two decades to transpire before the priest predator would be stopped, Brady may have followed a code and protocol in general use by his superiors. But he placed the reputation of the Church above *everything* else, including the welfare of innocent children, Browne argued. He bluntly condemned Brady's behaviour, making little in the way of allowances:

> Having twice interviewed the two abused boys and got them to tell in some detail the story of their abuse, an ordeal that must have caused those boys further trauma, he then insisted they swear an oath of secrecy, which, in itself, must have caused even more trauma. The claim that this oath of secrecy was to ensure that the investigatory process into the allegations of abuse was not compromised aggravates the gravity of what Brady did. It aggravates the gravity of what he did, because it is palpable nonsense.
>
> According to his own version of what happened, once Brady had concluded the second interview with the abused boys and then had administered the oath, that was the end of the process.
>
> Afterwards, he merely submitted his report to the relevant bishop, so the justification for administering the oath was gone by the time he prevailed upon the traumatized boys to swear it. Therefore, the only point of the oath at that stage was to protect the reputation of the church by concealing the abuse that had occurred.
>
> Séan Brady must know that his continuance in office will merely keep this issue concerning his conduct alive, thereby further damaging the institution he purports to serve.

Irish Times colleague Patsy McGarry concurs with Browne's analysis on the key points, including "the likelihood that his staying on will promote a further drip-drip of stories of abuse from those years, refocusing attention on him as leader of the Catholic Church in Ireland." He could find himself in the midst of further legal and media entanglements from which he will not be able to extricate himself. He could find himself a subject of interest by the courts, as Bernard Law did before Rome dispatched him to safer digs.

For sure, Brady is no Cardinal Groër.

But he is not Archbishop Penney, either.

Penney, unlike Law and Groër, was culpable by virtue of his oversights only. He was neither defiant nor evasive like Law, nor was he alleged to have committed abuse like Groër. Penney simply did the right thing following the release of the Winter Commission's report, a Commission he appointed and charged from the outset.

Brady's ill-advised tenacity – "I have decided to continue in my present role to play my part because I want to maintain the momentum towards better child safeguarding and, not alone that, momentum towards renewal of the faith which is essential" – stands in sharp contrast with the rugged pragmatism and no-nonsense approach of the Archbishop of Dublin and Primate of Ireland.

In an address entitled "The Future of the Catholic Church in Ireland," Diarmuid Martin reminded his listeners and readers (it was posted on the archdiocesan website and received a flood of hits) that "you cannot sound-byte your way out of a catastrophe." Only full disclosure, cooperation and contrition will work:

> Some will reply that sexual abuse by priests constitutes only a small percentage of the sexual abuse of children in our society in general. That is a fact. But that important fact should never appear in any way as an attempt to downplay the gravity of what took place in the Church of Christ. The Church is different; the Church is a place where children should be the subject of special protection and care. The Gospel presents children in a special light and reserves some of its most severe language for those who disregard or scandalize children in any way.

> In analyzing the past, it is important to remember that times may have been different and society and other professions may not have looked on the sexual abuse of children as they do today. It is hard however to understand why, in the management by Church authorities of cases of sexual abuse of children, the children themselves were for many years not even taken into the equation. Yes, in the culture of the day children were to be seen and not heard, but different from other professions Church leaders should have been more aware of the Gospel imperative to avoid harm to children, whose innocence was indicated by the Lord as a sign of the kingdom of God.

In other words, despite the statistics, the cultural tolerance and the general ignorance of and relative indifference to the welfare of children shown by society at large, the church is *different*. In other words, despite the similarities in governance between Church and society, shared management protocols and concern for reputation, the leadership of the Church must be different.

The failure to recognize these fundamental differences and the obligations that attend on such a recognition speaks to the ecclesial crisis and the very sundering of the Church's foundations. Although Diarmuid Martin is not prepared to allow for any evasion, subterfuge, unprincipled strategy or cheap rallying around the faith crusade to deflect the Church's commitment to redress and restitution, he realizes that the Church is larger than this crisis and that not all should be put on hold as the Irish Church deals with its history:

> The Catholic Church in Ireland is coming out of one of its most difficult moments in its history and the light at the end of the tunnel is still a long way off. The Catholic Church in Ireland will have to live with the grief of its past, which can and should never be forgotten or overlooked. There is no simple way of wiping the slate of the past clean, just to ease our feelings. Yet the Catholic Church in Ireland cannot be imprisoned in its past … Perhaps the future of the Church in Ireland will be one where we truly learn from the arrogance of our past and find anew a fragility which will allow the mercy and the compassion of Jesus to give us a change of heart and allow others through a very different Church to encounter something of that compassion and faith for their lives.

The above address was given to the Knights of Columbanus – a fervid, loyal Catholic lay fraternal order not known for its intellectual and spiritual temerity. They were stunned by Martin's unapologetic frankness. And his brother bishops were perplexed, if not angered, by his comment that he is discouraged and disheartened by the

... never-ending revelation about child sexual abuse and the disastrous way it was handled. There are still strong forces which would prefer that the truth did not emerge ... There are signs of subconscious denial on the part of many about the extent of the abuse which occurred within the Church of Jesus Christ in Ireland and how it was covered up. There are other signs of rejection of a sense of responsibility for what had happened. There are worrying signs that despite solid regulations and norms these are not being followed with the rigour required.

The bishops, as well as many priests, were distressed that Martin did not identify the "strong forces" opposed to the truth, thereby leaving a cloud hanging over all of them. Similarly, Ian Elliott, CEO of the National Board for the Safeguarding of Children, and the Board's chairman, John Morgan, sought clarification regarding the archbishop's remarks. Was he aware, for instance, of individuals who were not co-operating with the National Board's rules and requirements? If so, he could be liable for prosecution by withholding information.

Martin's subsequent press release indicated that he was speaking in only broad terms about the residual resistance to reform and openness, and not about new alliances or pockets of opposition. He named no names. But he refused to apologize for his forthrightness. He often shoots from the hip, frequently hits his targets, and just as frequently tastes the sting of the ricochet.

The *Sunday Independent* columnist Emer O'Kelly left no one in any doubt about where she stood on the media brouhaha over the Martin address. She spoke for many – secular, lapsed, and progressive Catholics:

> I wonder how many of the men listening to the Arch-
> bishop of Dublin Dr. Diarmuid Martin ... in the im-
> posing premises of the Knights of Columbanus in Ely
> Place in Dublin felt that he did not belong there.
>
> Did any of them, I wonder, go further and think
> that he did not even belong in the Roman Catholic
> Church that they know and believe in? Because I,
> for one, do not believe that Dr. Martin belongs in a
> Roman collar; and I do not believe that he belongs in
> the Roman Catholic Church. He is too good a man
> for any of them.

It is highly unlikely that Martin welcomed this form
of endorsement. It could not have won him plaudits
from his episcopal confreres, to say nothing of the papal
nuncio.

But it was a blessed change from the kind of environment cryptically captured by Galway's Ken Bruen, the
sardonic and popular writer of crime fiction who has been
taking the temperature of Ireland's rising anti-clericalism
in his Jack Taylor novels – *Priest, Cross, Sanctuary* – when
he notes: "Ireland had changed so much. A guy manhan-
dling a priest wasn't going to bring the cavalry; in fact,
it might well bring a lynch party." (*Sanctuary*, 98)

This is the world poignantly captured in the poem
"The O'Conor Don SJ" by spiritual writer Aidan Mathews, a world of "Seminaries silent. Churches sold. Priests
in prison/Children impaled. The annihilated father." It is
a world brought about, argues writer and Irish celebrity
John Waters in *Beyond Consolation: On How We Became Too
Clever for God ... and for Our Own Good*" by centuries of
institutional misapprehension of the Gospels:

The greatest abuse perpetrated by the Irish Church – and it was perpetrated by the Church as a whole rather than by a minority of abusers – was the promulgation of the idea that religion comes from the outside, that it is primarily an imposed system of control designed to police the instinctive desires of human beings. For 150 years this moralism was a form of idolatry in Irish society, which is to say that a long time ago the Irish Church broke the first commandment. (160)

Historians, theologians and ethicists will trace the Irish Church's penchant for a severe and puritanical morality to various sources, including the Penitentials, the decline of a uniquely Celtic ecclesiology, English subjugation, the Penal Laws, continental seminary training, Jansenism, Ultramontanism, as well as a wholesale cultural repudiation of a native Irish spirituality. As a result, the Irish Church became, like its Quebec counterpart, a tribal, clerical mini-state obsessed with its prerogatives, dignities and hegemony. It also became known for its fierce loyalty to Rome, its status as a virtually incomparable progenitor of vocations to the priestly and religious life, and its stronghold on the culture of its expanding diaspora.

But this Church, largely untouched by the reforms of the Second Vatican Council, and disinclined to take the laity seriously, succeeded nonetheless in creating through its vast missionary outreach a calibre of missioner remarkably well disposed to the best of current thinking in missiology, liberation theology, Catholic social thought and catechesis.

A heady and confusing mix, admittedly, and a key reminder that all that went before the meltdown was neither negative nor spirit-crushing. Nothing will be gained by opting for the Maximilien Robespierre approach to reform: eliminate history, evacuate the past, begin with Year One.

But perhaps nothing illustrates the climate of ecclesial crisis better than what transpired at the May 18, 2010, Requiem Mass for Martin Tierney. Tierney, the priest-founder of the Light of Christ lay community, author, retreat master and charismatic religious leader, was described in Michael Hurley's funeral homily as "the foremost prophetic voice in Irish religious life during the last forty years." With over 40 priest concelebrants and numerous bishops in attendance, Hurley exhorted all present at the funeral to heed Tierney's challenge to "re-imagine Church and parish life." Tierney outlined his strategy of "re-imagining" in an interview he gave shortly before his death. In the interview, he lambasted the bishops for their poverty of vision: "everything is centralized in the Church in Ireland, all power rests with the bishops and any initiative is cleverly suffocated by depriving it of oxygen. Whether it's in politics or in the Church where everything is centralized in an unaccountable elite it is ultimately doomed to failure: it simply can't breathe." He lamented the absence of any kind of pastoral strategy: "we're talking about clustering parishes, amalgamating dioceses, but there's no strategy. The bishops seem to just want to build structures that will keep everything going for the next few years or so. What sort of Church are we planning for fifty years from now, one hundred years from now? There has never been a strategy." He deplored the persistent failure to see the damage done by clericalism: "there are bishops up and down the country talking about clericalism and criticizing clericalism themselves. It's mind-boggling at times that they can't see it." And he sharply critiqued the stubborn opposition to actually implementing Vatican Council II and Code of Canon Law-inspired innovations such as parish councils and the empowering of lay people: "people say we must involve the laity or we must involve women, but that's not a plan, that's just a statement; if the Government tried to run the country based on statements and no action there'd be anarchy, yet we seem to think that it is okay to run the church on statements and speeches."

No holds barred.

And by one of the most respected priests in the country.

In other words, calls for reform are not exclusively the property of liberal lay groups, renegade theologians, victim-activists, legal advocates, newspaper columnists or disaffected Irish Catholics and bona fide anticlericals of long-standing reputation. Even parochial clergy with unimpeachable records of service and ecclesiastical fidelity are speaking up. One of these is the Abbot of Glenstal Abbey, Mark Patrick Hederman. His latest book, *Underground Cathedrals*, alerts Irish Catholics to the salutary fact that "there are moments in history when a people get a chance to re-invent their country" and in the process rejuvenate their Church.

And there are people – lay people – who are responding in significant numbers to the crisis rather than waiting for the bishops to show leadership that breaks them out of the stranglehold of their self-induced paralysis. People like the psychologist Bryan Maguire (abused himself by Father Donal Collins while at St. Peter's College), who has spearheaded the Voice of the Faithful in Ireland. The Voice of the Faithful first emerged in Boston following that archdiocese's devastating spate of allegations, court cases and settlements, culminating with the resignation of Bernard Law and his unseemly spiriting to Rome. Now they are in Ireland and a beacon of hope.

In an interview with *Irish Catholic's* Young Adults columnist Ben Conroy, Maguire sounds a refined and irenic psycho-theological note:

> The Gospel message is the most profound, multi-layered, multi-dimensional articulation of the connectedness between human suffering and our divine impulse that exists anywhere. And that is why the Church has to continue … It is only by attending to our woundedness that we come to know Jesus, and that we come to know the peace that he brings. It's not by shutting out the Great Scandal by getting beyond the abuse, that we are going to heal the Church.

The struggles of the Irish Church remind Canadian Catholics of the turmoil of the Quiet Revolution in 1960s Quebec and its reverberating aftermath: massive secularization of all the social service, health care and educational institutions; the drying up of religious vocations; plummeting attendance at Mass and other religious services; the marginalizing of religion as a constitutive factor in all social and political decision-making; and the reduction of a once vital presence to the status of a historical footnote, with empty churches, convents and monasteries becoming items of heritage and tourism interest only.

The evacuation of all religious symbolism and the wholesale rejection of a meaningful religious and cultural history have contributed in no small part to the various tensions and crises that have gripped Quebec society in a way that is disproportionate to the national average.

But there is vitality and a perduring spirituality in the Quebec Catholic Church to be found in its own "underground cathedrals." It has become a genuine counter-cultural sign, ripped from its Constantinian moorings, humbled, powerless, a voice aching to be heard in the larger cacophony of public sounds. And there are signs that it is working. But the restoration of the *ancien régime* is not in the cards, in spite of nostalgic dreams to the contrary.

Although the changes in the Quebec Church were not precipitated by the kind of clerical sex abuse issues boiling over in the Irish church, there are commonalities of history and religious culture, survival strategies over against British and Protestant rule, and a highly controlling clericalism that mark them as similar churches.

How the Canadian Catholic Church moves beyond the turbulent upheaval reignited by the Lahey affair, the Prince affair, the Windle affair, and so on, will be partly determined by how the Church diagnoses the complex array of causes that produced the crisis; how it structures its response once it has survived the initial shock waves; what vision it can articulate for a new, cleansed and reinvigorated ecclesial community; and what larger counsel and models it can offer the universal Church as it wrestles with a problem unprecedented in its scope in the post-Reformation Church.

Clericalism is the abuse of the power of the priesthood and should not be equated with the presbyterate. Clericalism exists as a structure, consciousness, and tribal and cultic stratum within the universal Church. It detracts from the effectiveness of the priestly ministry by virtue of its exalted self-regard, cultivated sense of privilege, instinct for self-perpetuation, and jealously guarded aura of holy distinctiveness. And it is the death knell of a flourishing, relevant and credible presbyterate.

The curse of clericalism, as Bishop Alexander Carter of Sault Ste Marie characterized it in a 1971 intervention to a Roman Synod of Bishops, is at the heart of the sex abuse crisis. Clerical power is realized in myriad forms in everyday parish life, and although many priests abjure its unsavoury exclusiveness and work comfortably with their lay partners, the clerical mentality is embedded in all strata of Catholic ecclesial life. The Winter Commission recognized the perils of clericalism. Various studies and investigations in England, the United States and Australia have identified clericalism as a major problem in the seminaries. Rectors such as Donald Cozzens have written about the "changing face of the priesthood" in ways that confront the working illusions that govern much of priestly training and the institutional denial that accompanies the psycho-sexual culture that thrives in many seminaries. Yet although various consultations and formal investigations have worked to impose discipline and integrity within the walls of clerical formation, the fundamental questions around clericalism persist.

One of the most egregious instances of clerical sex abuse uncovered in 2000–2001 is unrelated to pedophilia or pederasty. It concerned the systematic sexual exploitation of nuns by clerics in several African countries. Priests were known to seek out nuns for sexual gratification. The argument, as incredible as it may seem, was that if the sisters did not comply, the priests would be forced to solicit the favours of prostitutes, thereby exposing themselves to the risk of contracting HIV/AIDS. One superior-general who complained to her archbishop that 29 of her sisters had been impregnated by priests was relieved of her administrative responsibilities; the archbishop set up an alternative administration. While pregnant nuns are dismissed from their orders to face a life of potential destitution and assured humiliation, the priests who have fathered the children are surreptitiously relocated, sent abroad for study or put on extended retreat leave.

As Douglas R. Letson argues in his chapter "The Curse of Clericalism" in *Power and Peril: The Catholic Church at the Crossroads*,

> The official explanation for the abuse is rooted in cultural perceptions concerning the status of the priest in African society, the relative roles of men and women in society and in the Church, the superiority that accompanies education and the inferiority that accompanies poverty and ignorance, the conviction that celibacy as sexual abstinence is a social convention peculiar to Western culture, and the perception that having sexual relations with many women is an expression of power and status. It is a structure of power coupled with a naïve sense of obedience to male authority that is available to the impoverished African male in virtually no other form, since, as a candidate for the priesthood, the seminarian receives

an education from the Church that would almost certainly be otherwise unavailable to him.

With status comes power. With power comes responsibility. And with responsibility comes accountability. (p. 256)

The power associated with clericalism – a power of dominance, manipulation and sacralized authority that puts it outside the realm of accountability – runs counter to the liberating and enabling ministry of the priesthood. As Alexander Carter's brother Gerald Emmett – one-time Cardinal Archbishop of Toronto, a Council Father, and an esteemed catechist – mused in a series of oral interviews conducted as part of the research phase in the writing of his official biography, *My Father's Business,*

One of the interventions at the Second Vatican Council was by my brother who talked about the decree on the laity. He said that this conciliar document was born in original sin, the original sin of clericalism. He went on to develop the idea that we had misplaced the revelation which Jesus brought us because we insisted on postulating that the only leadership in many areas had to be in the hands of the clergy, the priest, or the religious orders. We had neglected the leadership of the laity.

I don't want to denigrate the priest in any way, but at the same time I believe that we are going to come out of the semi-darkness in which we find ourselves the better for the new light. If we hadn't had the Second Vatican Council we would be much worse off than we are.

The Council was the highpoint of my education in the Church. It changed my whole view of the Church. It changed my whole view of Christianity. Not that I was in heresy, but I had a great need of light and the four sessions of the Council I attended gave it to me. It was also a turning point in the history of the Church.

The Carter brother bishops were one in their detestation of clericalism. They identified it as a force or structure that worked against the effective call to discipleship of the laity, and therefore as a repository of deep resistance to the changes being heralded by the Council itself. This view reflects the awareness shared by many of the Council Fathers that the rightful incorporation of the laity in the life of the Church does not result in the diminishment of the role of the ministerial priesthood, but the extirpation of clericalism.

This point, in turn, brings us to consider what the Council taught about the Church itself. Prior to the Council, the concept of the Church as a *societas perfecta* was widely accepted. According to this perspective, we have everything we need in ourselves. All the necessary ingredients for salvation conformed nicely to the image of the Church as a besieged society: besieged by secularism, hostile Enlightenment thinkers, modernist threats to the integrity of doctrine, and such dangerous notions as democracy, religious freedom and a critical-historical approach to the biblical texts.

The Second Vatican Council did not spurn earlier definitions of the Church – previous dogmatic statements culled from history and the development of doctrine – nor did it supplant or supersede such ecclesiological teachings as can be found in Pius XII's *Mystici Corporis Christi*. Rather, the Council thought to focus on another dimension of ecclesial life, a dimension of life and meaning as Church that returned to both the scriptures and the writings of the Early Church Fathers: the idea of the church as a pilgrim people.

The Constitution on the Sacred Liturgy (*Sacrosanctum Concilium*) put it this way:

> The church is essentially both human and divine, visible but endowed with invisible realities, zealous in action and dedicated to contemplation, present in the world but as a pilgrim, so constituted that in her the human is directed toward and subordinated to the divine, the visible to the invisible, action to contemplation, and this present world to that city yet to come, the object of our quest. (# 2)

Further, the conciliar document on the laity, *Apostolicam Actuositatem*, acknowledges the common dignity of all the Church's members. This dignity, which derives from their "common grace of being God's children, the common call to perfection," underscored the rights and opportunities of the laity: to receive the spiritual goods of the Church; to express their views on Church matters; to initiate activities in the service of the Church; and to cooperate, where appropriate, in the ministry of the episcopate, including appointment to relevant ecclesiastical offices.

In the Constitution on the Church in the Modern World (*Gaudium et Spes*), and in the Dogmatic Constitution on the Church (*Lumen Gentium*), the Council Fathers articulated an understanding of the Church that is grounded in the notion of sacrament. They presented a view of the Church as a sign and instrument of intimate union with God: of the church, the *ekklesia* or assembly, as the People of God, a graced community, a pilgrim people, a communion people. In "The Ecclesiology of Vatican Council II" (*Origins*, April 22, 1999), the respected American ecclesiologist Joseph A. Komonchak outlines the challenges that Vatican II has set for theologians charged with implementing its teaching on the Church:

> The first is that of integrating the set of statements which lay out the two great dimensions of the church that come together in its single mysterious reality: the divine and the human. Since the council, in an understandable reaction to the concentration on institutional elements of the church, themselves often thought to exhaust the earthly, visible, human reality of the church, attention has focused on the distinct and transcendent dimensions of the church, particularly the communion in the divine life that is the church's deepest mystery. But that this is a dimension of the church is neglected when it is taken as a definition of the church itself or to exhaust its formal intelligibility.
>
> The church is not itself divine; it is a community of creatures blessed beyond merit with divine gifts, enabled beyond their abilities to respond with faith, hope and love to the divine offer. I sense the danger of a new monophysitism in ecclesiology when the human responses of faith, hope and love and the intersubjectivity they enable and embody are not considered constitutive of the church, and when it is forgotten that this communion is realized in a people of God still on pilgrimage in history.

The operative phrase, "still on pilgrimage in history," reminds us of the Church's – our – vulnerability, fragility, incompleteness, imperfection and tentativeness. We are a holy people aching into holiness. Our structures reflect our own innate capacities for rigidity, fear, defensiveness and tendency to idolatry.

Few appreciated the nature of change when it comes to Church customs, rituals and teachings better than John Henry Cardinal Newman. In his *Essay on the Development of Doctrine*, first published in 1845 (the year of his conversion to Catholicism) and republished in 1878 with extensive revisions, Newman likens change to a stream that is clearest near the spring:

> In time it enters upon strange territory; points of controversy alter their hearing; parties rise and fall around it; dangers and hopes appear in new relations; and old principles reappear under new forms. It changes with them in order to remain the same. In a higher world it is otherwise, but here below to live is to change, and to be perfect is to have changed often.

> If change is of the essence of living, then no person nor structure is immune to its creative and necessary enticements. To resist change is sometimes to atrophy, to die. And because the church – divine and human – is embodied in this world, change is critical to its lasting vitality and relevance.

Newman also understood the nascent dignity and importance of the laity as laity. At one point, when Newman's bishop, W.B. Ullathorne of Birmingham, asked him who precisely the laity are, he is said to have responded that the church "would look foolish without them."

In 1859, his *On Consulting the Faithful in Matters of Doctrine* appeared and Newman's reputation as a champion of the laity was secured. In this work he outlined his understanding of the role of the laity and their fundamental indispensability for an orthodox faith. He advanced his "dangerous" notion of the *sense of the faithful* or *sensus fidelium*, "a branch of evidence which it is natural or necessary for the Church to regard and consult, before she proceeds to any definition born from its intrinsic cogency."

In *On Consulting*, Newman demonstrated by way of a careful assemblage of relevant historical data the value of the *sensus fidelium*. The laity held firm when episcopal authority wavered and theological opinion collapsed into the din of Babel. There is a voice for the laity and there is a place for the laity, not only in articulating a sense of the faith but in providing an intelligent and critical reception of Church teaching.

> I think I am right in saying that the tradition of the Apostles, committed to the whole church in its various constituents and functions *per modum unis*, manifests itself variously at various times: sometimes by the mouth of the episcopacy, sometimes by the doctors, sometimes by the people, sometimes by liturgies, rites, ceremonies, and customs, by events, disputes, movements, and all those other phenomena which are comprised under the name of history. It follows that none of these channels of tradition may be treated with disrespect; granting at the same time fully, that the gift of discerning, discriminating, defining, promulgating, and enforcing any portion of that tradition resides solely in *Ecclesia docens* … I think certainly that the *Ecclesia docens* is more happy when she has …

enthusiastic partisans about her ... than when she cuts off the faithful from the study of her divine doctrines and the sympathy of her divine contemplations, and requires from them a *fides implicita* in her word, which in the educated classes will terminate in indifference, and in the poorer in superstition.

One can see why the authorities in the Roman curia, as well as other prominent converts, such as Manning, Ward, Faber and Talbot, would read Newman's work with rising disquiet. His final kick at this can, if you will, can be found in the appendix to the third edition of his *Arians of the Fourth Century*, wherein he reminds his readers of the visceral fidelity of the laity in contrast to the disabling fractiousness of the church leaders:

The episcopate, whose action was so prompt and concordant at Nicea on the rise of Arianism, did not, as a class or order of men, play a good part in the troubles consequent upon the Council; and the laity did. The Catholic people, in the length and breadth of Christendom, were the obstinate champions of Catholic truth, and the bishops were not ... on the whole, taking a wide view of history, we are obliged to say that the governing body of the church came short, and the governed were pre-eminent in faith, zeal, courage, and constancy.

Newman's defense of the laity, his understanding of the principle of change, and his trust in the organic living tradition of the Church should serve as beacons of direction in our dark and darkening time. To move forward as a Church we must recognize that in the issue of clerical sex abuse and the attendant credibility crisis, we have a stark and disturbing instance of the governing body of the Church coming up short. It is not enough to stand mute and seething while we witness what Donald Cozzens calls the "collapse of the Roman Catholic empire – not, I hope, of the Roman Catholic Church. Empires, whether temporal or ecclesial, no longer work."

Whether this is a time of empire dismantling or the death throes of clericalism, it is a time that requires change – demands change – if effective renewal is to take hold in the corridors of power, the chambers of decision-making

We need *structural* renewal.

Vatican II's document on the bishops, *Christus Dominus*, states clearly in chapter two that "it is greatly desired that in each diocese a pastoral commission will be established over which the diocesan bishop himself will preside and in which specially chosen clergy, Religious and lay people will participate. The duty of this commission will be to investigate and weigh pastoral undertakings and to formulate practical conclusion regarding them." Such a diocesan commission could be a particular or local instance of subsidiarity. Such a commission could serve as a legitimate and credible manifestation of genuine collaboration. Not an empty showcase; not a periodic body summoned under duress; not a council of deferential lay people keen on expressing their zeal and yet lamentably short of informed theological education. And such a commission could serve as a regular and open forum for the frank exchange of opinion, the sharing of diverse competencies, and all to the common end of advising the bishop in the exercise of his stewardship. In other words, see and value lay people as coequals, not subordinates to the clergy; see lay people as mature adults prepared to bring their charisms to the service of their Church, not interlopers poised to breach the clerical walls and wrest the power unto themselves.

Involve the laity in the education of priests from the outset. The more comfortable priests-in-formation are with the laity, and the more they appreciate the range of their gifts (it is not uncommon in many parishes in the Western Church to discover in the pews theologians and religious studies graduates who are better educated than their pastors), the more they will see them not as a threat to their own vocations but as fellow pilgrims.

Create and nurture a seminary environment that allows for the recognition of the complex factors that contribute to a healthy psycho-sexual maturation. It is not enough to employ various tests at the time of admission to determine an appropriate level of personal stability and adequacy for priesthood. An environment that acknowledges the many and diverse factors that contribute to an individual's sexual maturation will be sensitive to the mystery and beauty of sexuality, and not just its pathologies.

Foster a culture of transparency and accountability throughout all the levels of Church governance. Diocesan bishops are powerless to effect structural change in Rome, but they are free enough to enact legislation at the local level that will encourage a culture of forthright honesty. Such a culture does not deploy subterfuge in the interests of protecting the Church's reputation. Such a culture does not place as its key priority the avoidance of scandal. Such a culture does not neglect the innocent to insulate the powerful from moral culpability.

Establish periodic diocesan synods to address the challenges and threats to effective ministry peculiar to the region. Such pastoral synods should not be seen either as renegade incursions into the area of ecclesiastical authority, nor as occasions to subvert and foment, but rather as bona fide expressions of the spiritual commonwealth that is the Roman Catholic Church at its best and most apostolic. Provincial and national synods could emerge from the work of the local synods, although they would be infrequent (once a decade is ideal).

Ensure the public dissemination of annual diocesan reports that scrupulously measure the compliance of child safety policies. The creation and implementation of such policies should respect local diocesan autonomy, but should also be the result of national episcopal initiatives that are congruent with civil legislation. On such non-doctrinal matters, the local Ordinary's authority should be subordinate to the episcopal conference. In this regard, the weakening of the authority and value of national episcopal conferences – in great measure the result of Joseph Ratzinger's theological reservations over their validity – has proven to be a singular error. By centralizing oversight in the matter of clerical abuse, the Vatican has compromised the ability of individual bishops to act decisively and with alacrity, has compounded the confusion over canonical priorities versus civil ones, has prolonged the decision-making process and thus created greater opportunities for continued abuse, and has perpetuated the perception of clerical entitlement and discrete treatment. Ratzinger could not have made it clearer than he did in a 1985 statement: "Episcopal conferences have no theological basis, they do not belong to the structure of the Church, as willed by Christ, that cannot be eliminated; they have only a practical, concrete function ... No episcopal conference, as such, has a teaching mission; its documents have no weight of their own, save that of the consent given to them by the individual bishops." As pope, he has not given any sign that he intends to depart from his thinking on the validity and value of these conferences. What could have been a meaningful expression of the principle of collegiality has been bracketed as problematic, delimiting the authority of the local Ordinary, without serious theological warrant. This view is potentially intrusive in terms of immediate accountability to Rome by the bishops as bishops. The cost of neutering the episcopal conference as a legitimate organ of collegiality and policy implementation, as an instrument of solidarity among bishops, is proving to be a heavy one.

Establish a national forum to review, explore and implement the many recommendations that surface in *From Pain to Hope* and *Breach of Faith, Breach of Trust*. They are a national godsend, reflecting intense work by committed individuals representing a broad range of professional backgrounds. As Nuala Kenny, a pediatrician, faculty of medicine professor, bioethicist and Halifax Sister of Charity laments regarding the "unfinished business" of these reports,

> The work of Newfoundland's Winter Commission, on which I sat, and the subsequent work of the Canadian Conference of Catholic Bishops – *From Pain to Hope* and *Breach of Faith, Breach of Trust* – with which I was closely involved remains "unfinished business." These documents constitute a teachable moment.

The Canadian Church twenty years ago exhibited great courage when it addressed the issue of abuse – it struck lay-led panels and exercised unprecedented leadership. But it is time to reignite that bold courage and to shore up the strength of our convictions. If we persist in seeing this crisis as a person-specific issue, we are limited in our capacity for reform. Systemic analysis is critical and yet we still shy away from it. In that way the *whole* church becomes a victim.

To give one concrete example: is our approach as a church to sexuality too lofty? Is there a way for us as a church to update our approach, to provide a more pastoral and existential and less ontological and canonical approach?

Kenny's *cri de coeur* is rooted in years of personal and professional service to society and to the Church. Hers is not a rallying call for institutional dissent; it is a summons to change, open inquiry, grounded personalism, mature fidelity to the Gospel imperatives, and deep devotion to the communion of believers.

This view stands in marked contrast to the desiccated and lifeless structure that priest and spiritual writer Daniel O'Leary sees in desperate need of transformation. Writing in the January 16, 2010, issue of *The Tablet*, he says,

> The clerical model of church authority has drifted too far from the vision of the carpenter's son. Commentators refer to the idolatrous pull of power, privilege and possessions that subtly infect even the most religious organization when an isolating clericalism replaces a living servanthood ... Beyond the scandals, a radical reform of the whole Church – its essential purpose

and vision – is urgently needed. And this reformed Church will have much to say to the world. But first it must befriend it. The "secular" postmodern world is God's body too.

O'Leary's clarion call for a full reform will resonate with countless numbers of Catholics whose loyalty to the Church, deep faith in the tradition and regenerative capacity for hope speak to the maturity of their spirituality. Reformation is not demolition. But reformation does necessitate an honest, perhaps even searing, review of our institutional deficiencies, our collective failure to serve Jesus, our neglect of the implications of new knowledge, our fear of innovation.

If we are not to be doomed to repeat the sick patterns of the past, to withdraw into the faux safety of our citadel of resistance, to look fearfully onto the future, we will need to tackle our current ecclesiastical and moral meltdown as individuals, as local faith communities, as a national church and as the universal Catholic communion.

Undoubtedly, many efforts are under way to identify and root out the malpractices and dysfunctional structures of the immediate past. Such initiatives have been begun by local dioceses, national episcopal conferences, various Vatican dicasteries and the pope himself. The first and immediate lesson has been learned: we must clean up our act.

But as the recommendations of the various reports we have described indicate, there is much unfinished business.

And this is the hard part. A serious exploration of the ways and means that religious leaders have deployed, consciously or otherwise – to deal with the fallout of the scandals, to curtail the damage caused by the media blitz, to seek reconciliation with the abused, to offer compensation to the aggrieved, and to correct past pastoral practices that proved inadequate in the face of clerical misbehaviour of deplorable magnitude and gravity – needs to be done. In many cases it is being done, and with an impressive record of success. Even the much maligned Irish Church has a sterling record of policy implementation and compliance, of oversight and accountability. Compared to the protection of children provided by its government equivalents, the Church's efforts demonstrate a new level of earnestness and professionalism. So things are being done and with an uncustomary speed. Lessons learned.

But not quite.

The hard part is doing more than conducting reviews of past failures, establishing boards of inquiry, sending papal legates to perform the work of apostolic visitations, offering public apologies and creating blue ribbon committees to expedite the development of appropriate policies. These are all necessary, of course, and welcome.

But the "unfinished business" involves much more. It involves a determination to address the persistent structural pathologies that afflict the Church, a willingness to listen to the deeper cries for renewal, and an openness to the work of the Spirit, a work that has never been confined to the established order only.

In a September 2009, Gerald O'Collins delivered a public lecture at the Jesuit-run Heythrop College in the University of London. The Australian Jesuit scholar, emeritus professor of systematic theology at the Pontifical Gregorian University in Rome, prolific writer and esteemed priest identified seven dreams he had for the post-conciliar Church. His dream number five speaks especially to the current anguish around the restriction of all clerical ministries to men, and its possible remedy.

> I call my fifth dream "enriching ministries." Down the centuries the history of the Church has been blessed with the shining example of Christian men and women in various ministries such as the ministries of education and health care … The theme of ministries that enrich the Church and the world can open up sensitive issues. One of these is the issue of women being ordained to the diaconate. Many Catholic women do similar work to male deacons by their ministry as parish administrators and chaplains in schools, hospitals and prisons. These women are already performing more or less the same diaconal "service" as permanent male deacons. Why not ordain them to the permanent diaconate?

O'Collins has pressed this issue with the International Theological Commission. He takes pains to distinguish between ordination to the diaconate and ordination to the presbyterate. The role of women in one of the ordained ministries will add a dimension of presence and wellness that is missing in the Church. The level, intensity and breadth of the clerical sex abuse crisis would have been profoundly mitigated had women been more prominently engaged in the official life of the Church.

Admittedly, the issue of the priestly ordination of women is off limits as far as the Church is concerned.

The Church has ruled on the matter. Several times. *Roma locuta est; Roma finita est.* Or not.

Either way, such a debate – whether officially foreclosed or not – should not be allowed to eclipse the many other components that constitute the tapestry of this global crisis. Optional celibacy, declining access to regular celebration of the Eucharist, the generation of authentic ministries of collaboration, the dismantling of a culture of entitlement and secrecy, the demystifying of the ministerial priesthood, a reconsideration of the narrow rules for the appointment of bishops, a nurturing of a culture of transparency and episcopal accountability, the vigorous application of the ecclesial principles of collegiality and subsidiarity in all the operations of church governance – these, too, are part of our "unfinished business."

It may be true, to employ a salty Newfoundland nautical metaphor, that the church is like a sinking ship with her "arse out of 'en, the stern full of water and we're going down." But most Catholics would prefer to see the current breakdown of structure and credibility as a summons to Christian reform. It is towards this kind of reform that the Irish-Canadian historian and classicist Mary Malone, in "And, of Course, Women" in *Doctrine and Life* (Summer 2010), calls us to eschew as "a kind of male generic reform that still is blind to the other half of the tradition, that half inhabited by women down the Christian centuries. Let it be a reform that is post-patriarchal and post-androcentric in both its human and divine aspects. Let it be as eager for the death of old forms as it is for the generation of the new."

Such a radical revisioning of Catholic ecclesiology is likely to have little support among the hierarchy for the foreseeable future. What can inspire, serve as a corrective and implant that sense of hope so critical for renewal *and* reform is a Catholic spirituality grounded in an authentic humility and in a compassionate anthropology.

In his stunningly fair, non-vindictive and insightful novel *The Long Run*, Newfoundlander Leo Furey recreated the immediacy and the terror of the Mount Cashel nightmare with his fictional Mount Kildare orphanage for boys. His treatment, unlike that of filmmaker John Smith in *The Boys of St. Vincent*, is a more nuanced glimpse of life "inside."

Furey sets his novel during the period between the autumn of 1961 and the summer of 1962. Although he captures something of the whirligig of sexual repression, sexual anxiety, sexual exploration and curiosity that together define the contortions and upheavals of the teenage male, the novel also evokes the boys' world of Mount Kildare, a world awash in homesickness, institutional discipline, strategies of coping (reminiscent of the numerous public school memoirs of unhappy Englishmen) and, of course, feelings of attachment and bonding.

In a scene, the only one of its kind, where the devastating pathology of sexual predation is portrayed with gripping intensity, the impact on the reader is magnified by the comparative economy of expression. Aiden Carmichael, the novel's narrator, paints the scene:

> The next morning at breakfast we tell Blackie [the leader] what happened, and he says he isn't surprised there's a night walker. And he isn't surprised that he

stopped at Nowlan's bed either. He says he knew as much. "Nowlan's goin to the infirmary a lot. Always sick. No, not sick, sad."

"But if Nowlan isn't sick, if he's just sad, why's he go to the infirmary all the time? Does he always get the spells?" I ask.

"Nowlan's always sad," Oberstein [the savant] says. "That's a kind of sickness, always being sad."

"It's deep ... deep inside him," Blackie says. "It's soulful, a different kind of sickness, the sadness sickness." (p. 151)

Furey's portrait of the religious brothers who operate the school is intelligent and measured, discriminating and scrupulously considered. He refuses the easy appeal of stereotyping and recognizes that the brothers run the gamut from the seriously dysfunctional to the idealistic and empathetic. There are the sociopaths and there are the saints. But mostly they are injured men – lonely, addicted to power, living out their lives in a Church that is as much a prison as a gateway to holiness.

Furey's "sadness sickness" has penetrated the very pores of the Church, and it has spread widely. Another Canadian, Ronald Rolheiser, offered his prescient prognosis in his June 22, 2002, syndicated column, years before the worst was to unfold on the global scene:

We have to be prepared for a season, perhaps a long one, of continued pain and embarrassment and a further erosion of trust. We need to accept this without self-pity and without being overly self-protective. Partly we are ill (though everyone is) and, like a virus that has infected the body, this has to run its course and the body, in fever and weakness, has to build up a new immune system. In a situation like this, there is only one thing to do and the *Book of Lamentations* spells it out graphically: "Put your mouth to the dust and wait."

As the Roman Catholic Church builds up a "new immune system" – a system marked by transparency, openness to correction, institutional humility and zeal for purification – it is important to retain a perspective that is historical, proportionate and free from polemical posturing and ideological rigidity.

Perhaps there is no better source alive who can remind us of the essential truth rooted in the scriptures, mediated in the best traditions of the Church, and a hallmark of our christocentric humanism than philosopher, activist and spiritual writer Jean Vanier:

> a human being is more than the power or capacity to think and to perform. There is a gentle person of love hidden in the child within the adult. The heart is the place where we meet others, suffer, and rejoice with them. It is the place where we can identify and be in solidarity with them. Whenever we love, we are not alone.

> The heart is the place of our "oneness" with others. (*Becoming Human*, 1988, p. 86)

When we remember the centrality of the heart, we will then understand Jesus' injunction "to suffer the children to come unto me," and the Gospel-driven imperative and judgment that accompanies his words.

Afterword

Sister Nuala Kenny, OC, MD, FRCP(C)
Ethics & Health Policy Advisor,
Catholic Health Alliance of Canada

The breaking story of the arrest of Raymond Lahey came at me from the car radio with a jolt. I, along with many others, had thought sympathetically that he had resigned as Bishop of Antigonish because he suffered from stress or depression after dealing with the abuse settlement in the diocese of Antigonish. His arrest on charges of owning and importing child pornography changed everything for me. I had to pull off to the side of the road for fear of being sick.

In an unprecedented experience of flashback, I was back in the Burin Peninsula of Newfoundland in 1989 as a member of the Archdiocesan Commission of Inquiry on Clergy Sexual Abuse (the Winter Commission). I felt again the pain and distress of that time with both Mount Cashel and priestly betrayal. The Commission met with members of a parish in which James Hickey, then incarcerated, had molested young boys. We listened to their stories of anguish and devastation. I saw before me one older man, a craggy and weather-worn fisherman, who wept as he told us of the violation of a much-loved nephew and his anger for Hickey and for the Church itself. Once more I felt my own struggle to control myself as the man said he had not been able to talk to the God, who had been the centre of his life, since he heard of the atrocity. He doubted he would ever again.

As a pediatrician who knew something about the horrors of child abuse and a Roman Catholic religious Sister, I found the Newfoundland Commission to be the most difficult experience of my life. Horrible things were being done to vulnerable children and youth by priests of the Church to which I had given my life. The damage done to these victims was far more serious than that by other trusted figures because the perpetrators were priests of God.

Despite the personal difficulty, I was proud of the work we did in Newfoundland and of the subsequent work by the Canadian Conference of Catholic Bishops' Ad Hoc Committee on Sexual Abuse, where I served for another two years as the link to the Newfoundland experience.

However, I have always been aware that there was "unfinished business" here. The question from Chapter Five of the Newfoundland report – "Why did this happen?" – was always with me. In that chapter we rejected simple single causes and made an attempt to identify what we called "systemic factors" at work: "power, education, sexuality, support of priests, management and avoidance of scandal." While I now have a somewhat different analysis of these factors, I know more surely than ever before that until and unless we take into account these cultural and systemic factors, the story of clergy sexual abuse in the Catholic Church will be never-ending. And the victims will not only be the vulnerable young, but all faithful priests and bishops and, indeed, all faithful Catholics.

In this tragic yet challenging book, Higgins and Kavanagh demonstrate the importance of story: who tells it; from what perspective it is told; who is hero and who is villain; how resolution is achieved. To date, the story of media headlines and of the Church's response has been one of individual sins and failures – of sexual predators and weak, sexually conflicted perpetrators, and of bishops who mishandled, denied, minimized the harm or chose to protect image and institution over vulnerable victims.

For me, and for a growing number of others who love the Church of Christ but not the un-Christlike institution it has too often become, there is another deeper, complex and challenging story yet to be written. The "unfinished business" of the Canadian Church and, indeed, the universal Church is the story of the systemic and cultural factors that allowed this situation to happen. These are the factors in need of deep, communal, open and accountable examination of conscience by all the baptized faithful, lay and ordained. What is it about us as a Church and the way we are with each other and for the world that has allowed these atrocities to go on for as long and as widely as they have? As someone who is trained in medicine, I believe that unless and until we understand the root causes of the clergy sexual abuse crisis, we are like a doctor treating symptoms while the deeper and deadly pathology saps energy and health, and ultimately kills.

Only part one of a tragic trilogy has been written to date. It contains the stories of sexual abuse by Roman Catholic clergy, with particular attention to the abuse of children and adolescents.

Part two is the story in urgent need of writing here and now. This is the story of the deeper pathology, the systemic and cultural factors that allowed abuse to occur. As I have returned to this issue in ways unimagined during the Newfoundland and Canadian Conference of Catholic Bishops' work in the early 1990s, much has been written. While the Newfoundland list of factors in need of study is still basically valid – "power, education, sexuality, support of priests, management and avoidance of scandal" – I have come to a more refined understanding of the systemic and cultural factors at work. Clearly, irresponsible management and a primary commitment to avoid scandal have resulted in the greatest scandal in the history of the modern Church. The Church today is, indeed, a "sign of contradiction," but not that envisioned by the cross of Christ. Protocols and seminary screening and formation have improved significantly and are crucial givens. We must now find a way to write the stories of at least three deeply inter-related and negatively reinforcing systemic/cultural issues: clericalism, sexuality, and some key theological concepts and beliefs.

Clericalism over priesthood; clericalism disempowering the laity

Coming from the deeply hierarchical world of academic medicine, I know that all institutions have a clergy – that is, an organizational structure with differentiation of powers, knowledge and status. The evil of clericalism exists when there is automatic status, protection of image and institution, resistance to critique and change, secrecy, non-accountability and, ultimately, loss of both the sense of the fundamental call and commitment to those whom they serve. How has clericalism fostered the silence and denial central to clergy abuse?

Clericalism is totally in contrast with priesthood understood first and foremost as the priesthood of all the baptized. It is in total opposition to the humility, mercy and servant leadership of the Lord Jesus. Clericalism has profoundly negative consequences for the roles and responsibility of the laity in the life and actions of the Church. How has clericalism fostered abrogation of responsibility for the abuse crisis by the laity? Clericalism has had devastating consequences for the real, loving support of today's priests and bishops by the faithful; you can't give tough love to a perfect, distant man on a pedestal! How does mandatory celibacy complicate these issues in its consequences for psycho-social development, intimacy, and loving, mutually giving relationships?

Sexuality – confused, conflicted and rejected

Issues of both sexual theology and sexual practice are background for the abuse crisis. On the one hand, Catholicism has an impossibly ideal set of magisterial statements on marriage, virginity and sexuality; on the other hand, we have a general perception of Catholic sexual morality as "dirty," secret and negative. Morality is dominated by sexuality. Yet, it is written by older celibate men with no real experience of the joys and pains of happy married life. What is the real effect on the abuse crisis of the exclusion of women, who rarely offend sexually against children, from the centre of Church life?

The contradictions at work in this area are the real context for the abuse crisis. Ever since the rejection of *sensus fidelium* in the *Humanae Vitae* decision on contraception, there has been a rift between the Church's teaching and practice. Moreover, a high population of priests are homosexual in a Church that understands homosexuality as disordered. How has this culture of contradiction and rejection of Church teaching facilitated the abuse crisis?

Some theological concerns

There are a number of important theological issues needing exploration. What ecclesiology or understanding of the Church has facilitated the crisis? How has the understanding of morality as a set of rules rather than formation of persons into the mind of Christ abetted the situation? Has the focus on sin and forgiveness, rather than crime and punishment, distorted our sense of justice?

The final story

The third and final book in this trilogy will be written only after we respond to these and other key questions. Higgins and Kavanagh rightly point out that there are competing analyses of why all this has become the crisis it is. "Conservatives" blame the Second Vatican Council; "liberals" blame the failure of adoption of the Second Vatican Council's vision of the Church. The abuse crisis can be a proxy for other agendas. Will the next story be one of renewal and rededication to the

Gospel that transcends these differences? A growing number of Church leaders seem to "get" the magnitude of the task at hand. My own bishop, Anthony Mancini, has asked, "Is this a time of purification or is it nothing more than devastation?" That *is* the question.

Diarmuid Martin, Archbishop of Dublin and Primate of Ireland, has said,

> We must face the truth of the past; repent it; make good the damage done. And yet we must move forward day by day along the painful path of renewal, knowing that it is only when our human misery encounters face-to-face the liberating mercy of God that our Church will be truly restored and enriched.

A story of liberating mercy and real renewal would indeed be the story of the Church of Christ.

Bibliography

Barry, Jason. *Lead Us Not into Temptation: Catholic Priests and the Sexual Abuse of Children.* Urbana and Chicago: University of Illinois Press, 2000.

Bottum, Joseph. "The Cost of Father Maciel." *First Things: A Monthly Journal of Religion & Public Life* 204 (2010)

Bruni, Frank and Elinor Burkett. *A Gospel of Shame: Children, Sexual Abuse, and the Catholic Church.* New York: Perennial, 2002.

Callahan, Sidney. "The Church's Gordian Knot." *Commonweal* (Sept. 10, 1999).

Carroll, James. *Practicing Catholic.* New York: Houghton Mifflin Harcourt, 2009.

Chinnici, Joseph P. *When Values Collide: The Catholic Church, Sexual Abuse, and the Challenges of Leadership.* Maryknoll, NY: Orbis Books, 2010.

Cozzens, Donald B. *The Changing Face of the Priesthood.* Collegeville, MN: Liturgical Press, 2000.

————. *Sacred Silence: Denial and the Crisis in the Church.* Collegeville, MN: Liturgical Press, 2002.

DeCosse, David E. "Freedom of the Press and Catholic Social Thought: Reflections on the Sexual Abuse Scandal in the Catholic Church in the United States." *Theological Studies* 68.4 (2007).

Dominian, Jack. *Proposals for a New Sexual Ethic*. London: Darton, Longman and Todd, 1977.

———. "Person to Person: Christian Marriage in a Changing World." *The Tablet* (Feb. 4, 1984).

———. "The Use of Sex: Christian Marriage in a Changing World." The Tablet (Feb. 11, 1984).

———. "Sexuality: From Law and Biology to Love and Person." *Grail: An Ecumenical Journal* 4.3 (1988).

Donnelly, Susie and Tom Inglis. "The Media and the Catholic Church in Ireland: Reporting Clerical Child Sex Abuse." *Journal of Contemporary Religion* 25.1 (2010).

Dorais, Michel. *Don't Tell: The Sexual Abuse of Boys*. Translated by Isabel Denholm Meyer. Montreal: McGill-Queen's University Press, 2002.

Doyle, Thomas P. "The Spiritual Trauma Experienced by Victims of Sexual Abuse by Catholic Clergy." *Pastoral Psychology* 58.3 (2009).

Erlandson, Gregory and Matthew Bunson. *Pope Benedict XVI and the Sexual Abuse Crisis: Working for Reform and Renewal*. Huntington, IN: Our Sunday Visitor Publishing Division, 2010.

Formicola, Jo Renee. "The Further Legal Consequences of Catholic Clerical Sexual Abuse." *Journal of Church and State* 49.3 (2007).

Fox, Thomas C. *Sexuality and Catholicism*. New York: George Braziller, 1995.

Friscolanti, Michael. "The Truth about Priests." *Maclean's* (Dec. 1, 2009).

Ghosh, Bobby, Jeff Israely and Tristana Moore. "Sins of the Fathers." *Time* 175.12 (2010).

Guindon, André. *The Sexual Language: An Essay in Moral Theology*. Ottawa: University of Ottawa Press, 1976.

―――. *The Sexual Creators: An Ethical Proposal for Concerned Christians*. Boston: University Press of America, 1986.

―――. *Moral Development, Ethics and Faith*. Ottawa: Novalis, 1992.

Hemingway, Mollie Ziegler. "More Emphasis on Confessing Might Have Helped." *Wall Street Journal – Eastern Edition* (June 4, 2010).

Higgins, Michael W. "Catholics in Shock." *The Tablet*. (Sept. 22, 1990). Reprinted with permission.

―――. "Focus on Sexual Abuse." *The Tablet*. (Feb. 13, 1993). Reprinted with permission.

Investigative Staff of the *Boston Globe*. *Betrayal: The Crisis in the Catholic Church*. Boston: Little, Brown and Company, 2002.

Israely, Jeff and Howard Chua-Eoan. "The Trial of Benedict XVI." *Time* 175.22 (2010).

Jenkins, Philip. *Pedophiles and Priests: Anatomy of a Contemporary Crisis*. New York: Oxford University Press, 1996.

Kane, Michael N. "Investigating Attitudes of Catholic Priests Toward the Media and the US Conference of Catholic Bishops Response to the Sexual Abuse Scandals of 2002." *Mental Health, Religion & Culture* 11.6 (2008).

Levine, Judith. *Harmful to Minors: The Perils of Protecting Children from Sex.* University of Minnesota Press, 2002.

Loftus, John Allan. *Understanding Sexual Misconduct by Clergy: A Handbook for Ministers.* Washington: Pastoral Press, 1994.

―――. "Before Dallas: The U.S. Bishops' Response to Clergy Sexual Abuse of Children." *Theological Studies* 70.1 (2009).

McHugh, Jim. "An Abuse of Power, a Betrayal of Trust: The Emperor Has No Clothes." *Grail: An Ecumenical Journal* 7:2 (1991).

McLaughlin, Megan. "The Bishop in the Bedroom: Witnessing Episcopal Sexuality in an Age of Reform." *Journal of the History of Sexuality* 19.1 (2010).

McMackin, Robert A., Terence M. Keane and Paul M. Kline. *Understanding the Impact of Clergy Sexual Abuse: Betrayal and Recovery.* London: Routledge, 2009.

Plante, Thomas G. *Bless Me Father for I Have Sinned: Perspectives on Sexual Abuse Committed by Roman Catholic Priests.* Westport, CT: Praeger, 1999.

―――. *Sins Against the Innocents: Sexual Abuse by Priests and the Role of the Catholic Church.* Westport, CT: Greenwood, 2004.

Roberts, Tom. "Some Bishops Questioning Clerical Culture." *National Catholic Reporter* 46.22 (2010).

Rossetti, Stephen J. *Slayer of the Soul: Child Sexual Abuse and the Catholic Church.* Mystic, CT: Twenty-Third Publications, 1990.

————. *A Tragic Grace: The Catholic Church and Sexual Abuse.* Collegeville, MN: Liturgical Press, 1996.

Sipe, Richard A.W. *Sex, Priests and Power: Anatomy of a Crisis.* New York: Brunner/Mazel, 1995.

Turner, Darrell. "Litigating Clergy Sex Abuse." *National Catholic Reporter* 44.29 (2008).

Transcontinental
PRINTING
IMPRIMERIE GAGNÉ

PRINTED IN CANADA